The
Feng Shui
Cookbook

The Feng Shui Cookbook

Creating Health
and Harmony
In Your Kitchen

ELIZABETH MILES

ILLUSTRATIONS BY
ROLAND ROSENCRANZ

A Birch Lane Press Book
Published by
Carol Publishing Group

A Birch Lane Press Book
Published by Carol Publishing Group
Birch Lane Press is a registered trademark of Carol Communications, Inc.

Editorial, sales and distribution, rights and permissions inquiries should be addressed to
Carol Publishing Group, 120 Enterprise Avenue, Secaucus, N.J. 07094.

In Canada: Canadian Manda Group, One Atlantic Avenue, Suite 105, Toronto,
Ontario M6K 3E7

Carol Publishing books may be purchased in bulk at special discounts for sales
promotion, fundraising, or educational purposes. Special editions can be created to
specifications. For details, contact Special Sales Department, 120 Enterprise Avenue,
Secaucus, N.J. 07094.

Designed by Andrew B. Gardner

Manufactured in the United States of America
10 9 8 7 6 5 4 3 2 1

Library of Congress Cataloging-in-Publication Data
Miles, Elizabeth.
The Feng Shui cookbook : creating health and harmony in your
kitchen / Elizabeth Miles.
p.   cm.
"A Birch Lane book."
Includes bibliographical references and index.
ISBN 1-55972-465-X
1. Nutrition.   2. Feng-shui.   3. Cookery, Chinese.   I. Title.
RA784.M485   1998
613.2—dc21   98-6446
CIP

Chinese philosophy holds that life force,
or qi, comes from breath and food.
The Feng Shui Cookbook is a guide to feeding your
life force in the daily act of cooking and eating.

Contents

Acknowledgments

This book draws upon centuries of work by feng shui masters, I Ching scholars, and Chinese medical doctors. I am deeply appreciative of the writings and wisdom of generations of people who have brought this ancient knowledge into the present, and for the emissaries in many fields who have shared feng shui and Asian foodways with the world.

Thanks to those who put their palates and qi on the line by helping perfect the feng shui recipes in their own kitchens: Lindsay Clare, Jim Cypherd, Deenya Rabius and Alex Wilson, Rachel Razo and Peter Gust, and Sarah and Arthur Schiller. Thank you to Roger Hyde, who drove me in his 1970 Buick Electra to the used-book store where I found my Bollingen edition of the I Ching, and thus became a sort of spiritual godfather to *The Feng Shui Cookbook*.

Thank you to my editor, Carrie Nichols Cantor, who spotted the essence of the work and helped me reveal it with a warm heart, good words, and clear vision.

Roland Rosencranz invested far more talent and artistic insight in the book's illustrations than I deserved; thank you for breathing life and sight into these images.

Many thanks and a thumbs-up to Betsy Amster, my agent and mentor, whose optimism, tenacity, literary skills, and excellent qi make me feel like a lucky player on a winning team.

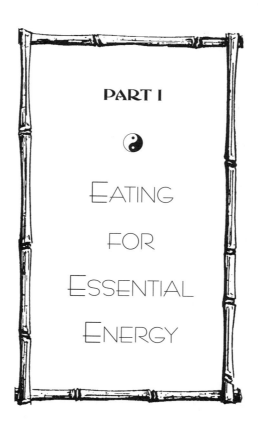

PART I

EATING

FOR

ESSENTIAL

ENERGY

Introduction

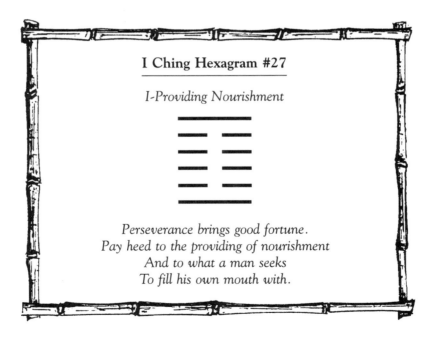

I Ching Hexagram #27

I-Providing Nourishment

Perseverance brings good fortune.
Pay heed to the providing of nourishment
And to what a man seeks
To fill his own mouth with.

For thousands of years, China has maintained a great civilization and one of the world's healthiest populations on the fundamental idea of *qi* (pronounced "chee"): the essential energy, or life force, that flows through people and the natural world. Perhaps as early as the fourth century B.C., Chinese qi masters were applying a unified body of *yin-yang* theory to channel the outer energy of the environment and the inner energy of individuals for optimal health and productivity.

The Feng Shui Cookbook (pronounced *fung-shway*) draws on this ancient wisdom to show how you can utilize the principles of yin-yang balance in your kitchen and your cooking to eat for essential energy. The design guidelines, recipes, and food-for-thought notes harness the powers of yin and yang to relax you when you're stressed, stimulate you when you're tired, bring out your best personality traits or the characteristics you need for a particular situation, and tap your potential in the areas of career, wealth, family, health, and social connections. You'll learn how to eat for wisdom, honesty, conviction, motivation, and forgiveness . . . and to strengthen, nourish, stimulate, concentrate, or cleanse your qi. You'll even discover how food can help you express joy, grief, anger, fear, and wonder. *The Feng Shui Cookbook* opens the door to an adventure in the ancient art and science of eating that can feed your essential energy for better health, greater prosperity, and a fresh view of pleasure at the table.

WIND AND WATER

The Chinese practice of environmental design known as *feng shui* translates as "wind and water," the forces that embody the flow and transformation of energy in the natural world. Tens of centuries ago, wind and water were the best friends and worst enemies of the agricultural society that populated China. Cold north winds sent hardship and disease, but soft southern breezes brought fresh, life-giving air. Rivers provided vital water for people, crops, and livestock when they stayed within their banks, but they devastated and killed during their frequent floods. Over time, people observed that wind and water determined the very topography of the land they worked and lived on. Their respect for both the life-sustaining and the life-threatening energy of these forces evolved into the art of feng shui.

Feng shui is the ecology of flow, the architecture of energy. Based on the idea that

good fortune results when people live in balance with their environments and their inner natures, feng shui has been praised as an environmentally sound practice that emphasizes respecting rather than tampering with nature. Today, this ancient and intuitive idea is so forgotten as to seem revolutionary.

As an environmental and spatial practice, feng shui's principles have been shown to predate and predict modern tenets of topography, geography, geology, climatology, hydrology, soil science, urban planning, architecture, building construction, and interior design. Its central doctrine of balance between yin and yang may be rooted in the first known discovery of the earth's magnetic poles by the Chinese, sometime around the fourth century B.C. In the human body, feng shui's concepts of qi and balance have much in common with contemporary nutrition and medicine. In short, feng shui is a time-honored way to tap into and balance the energy of all things for better health, relationships, and prosperity.

Wind and water represent the flow of energy in the natural world. *The Feng Shui Cookbook* helps you harness the flow of energy provided by food, and control the changes it enacts within you.

Feng Shui and the I Ching

The philosophical and cosmological basis of feng shui lies in the three-thousand-year-old text of the *I Ching,* or Book of Changes. The oldest surviving divinatory system in the world, the "I" (pronounced like the letter "e") was the first work to define and apply the balancing principles of yin and yang. It remains the foundation of Chinese thought, including feng shui and nutritional medicine.

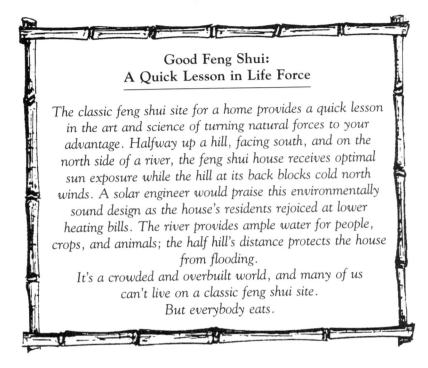

Good Feng Shui: A Quick Lesson in Life Force

The classic feng shui site for a home provides a quick lesson in the art and science of turning natural forces to your advantage. Halfway up a hill, facing south, and on the north side of a river, the feng shui house receives optimal sun exposure while the hill at its back blocks cold north winds. A solar engineer would praise this environmentally sound design as the house's residents rejoiced at lower heating bills. The river provides ample water for people, crops, and animals; the half hill's distance protects the house from flooding.

It's a crowded and overbuilt world, and many of us can't live on a classic feng shui site.

But everybody eats.

The yin-yang theory set forth in the I Ching proposes that opposites flow from each other, like the positive and negative forces of a magnet, and that the cyclical change created by this oppositional flow is both natural and beneficial. The life essence that results from the balance of yin and yang is qi, which animates all things to link humankind and nature, spirit and substance, mind and body.

The I Ching's sixty-four hexagrams, six-line diagrams depicting all the possible combinations of yin (broken lines) and yang (solid lines), present pragmatic strategies for the full range of dynamics and decisions that human life presents. Serving as a sort of bible for personal growth, social interactions, science, politics, and spirituality in Chinese culture, the I

Ching is the theoretical fountainhead for the practice of feng shui. All the concepts you'll encounter in this book—yin, yang, the Five Elements, the meaning of the cardinal directions, colors, seasons, and so forth—were first outlined by this ancient text.

The I Ching also serves as the basis for the tenets of Chinese nutritional medicine. Its ideas of balance between yin and yang and the powers of the Five Elements underlie Chinese theories about how food works in the body and mind and achieves aesthetic success. Some of the oracle's hexagrams directly depict food and eating as images for various life situations. These I Ching hexagrams head each chapter of this book as a reminder that the notion of nourishment has long been central to the venerable and vital tradition of balanced living.

You need not be an I Ching scholar to benefit from the wisdom of its text. Feng shui is the practical application of the I Ching in daily life, and with *The Feng Shui Cookbook*, you'll learn how to enact the I's principles every time you eat, feeding your life force with the wisdom of the world's most ancient oracle.

Qi

To the human organism, there are two sources of qi: breath and food.

Good *sheng qi* derives from the perfect balance of yin and yang energy. This good qi, born of balance, is alive and generates growth and good health. *Sha qi*, on the other hand, comes from yin-yang imbalance and acts as a destructive force. To enjoy the health

and prosperity that good qi provides, you must balance the environment around you—figuratively, the air you breathe—and the food you eat.

Food's vital role in creating essential energy is graphically represented by the Chinese pictograph for the word *qi*: the character for rice combined with a radical for rising vapors. The image of cooking rice *is* qi.

The role of yin-yang balance and qi in human health was first explored in *The Yellow*

S

Li

Fame / Rank

Fire: red, bitter

Suan

Wealth

blue, purple, red

Kuen

Marriage

red, pink, white

Jen

Family / Health

Wood: green, sour

E

W

Dwei

Children

Metal: white, hot

Earth

sweet yellow

Gen

Knowledge

black, blue, green

Chagan

Helpful People

white, gray, black

Kan

Career

Water: black, salty

N

Emperor's Manual of Corporeal Medicine, a second-century B.C. text attributed to the ruling emperor of the time. The manual documents that Chinese physicians were the first in the world to discover that blood circulates in the body (Europe trailed in this observation by nearly two thousand years). Accompanying this discovery was the proposal that just as the heart pumps blood, so the lungs pump qi. Blood is yin, qi is yang, and they are mutually dependent.

Within the body, qi can ascend and descend, contract and expand. When properly balanced and flowing, it protects the body from invaders. But when your qi becomes stagnant, depleted, or excessive, you become subject to disease.

The Chinese were also the first to recognize *circadian rhythms* (described in the *Yellow Emperor's Manual*), or the biological clock that governs your energy level, body temperature, brain chemistry, and so forth throughout the day. The idea of qi is inextricably bound up with the medical reality that people must maintain balance even in a constant state of change in order to be productive and healthy, and thus financially, socially, and spiritually successful.

In the world around us, pollution and diminishing resources reveal the imbalance of our external qi, while startling rates of diet- and lifestyle-related diseases demonstrate the widespread disruption of personal qi within individuals. Feng shui and Chinese medicine operate on the axiom that the body, mind, and external environment are constantly influencing one another. In order to achieve personal or social health and prosperity, we must create an environment of clean air and abundant, nourishing food—and then internalize that essential energy with every breath and bite.

THE FENG SHUI KITCHEN BA GUA

One of the basic tools of feng shui is the *ba gua,* an octagon that summarizes all of the principles of yin-yang balance found in the I Ching. This spatial and conceptual instrument is built upon the I Ching's eight trigrams (the three-line components of the hexagrams) to portray all the basic wants and needs of people on each of its eight sides, or *guas*. When the guas of the octagon are in balance, you enjoy optimal qi.

The Chinese venerate the south, source of life-giving sunshine, so much that they place this direction at the top of the ba gua and mark it with the royal color red. Each of the

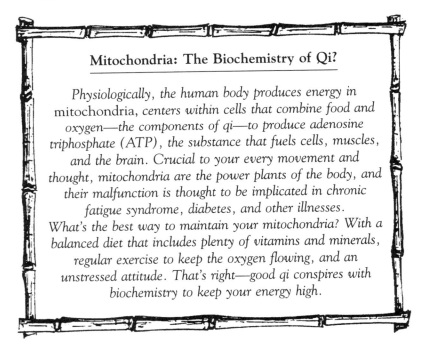

Mitochondria: The Biochemistry of Qi?

Physiologically, the human body produces energy in mitochondria, *centers within cells that combine food and oxygen—the components of qi—to produce adenosine triphosphate (ATP), the substance that fuels cells, muscles, and the brain. Crucial to your every movement and thought, mitochondria are the power plants of the body, and their malfunction is thought to be implicated in chronic fatigue syndrome, diabetes, and other illnesses.*
What's the best way to maintain your mitochondria? With a balanced diet that includes plenty of vitamins and minerals, regular exercise to keep the oxygen flowing, and an unstressed attitude. That's right—good qi conspires with biochemistry to keep your energy high.

four cardinal directions, along with the octagon's center, represents one of the Five Elements, which in turn are associated with life situations, colors, and the Five Flavors recognized by Chinese cuisine.

The Ba Gua and Your Environment

Feng shui practitioners use the ba gua to determine how to maximize the environmental qi of a space, whether it's a room, house, or property. By aligning the directions indicated on the octagon with those of the space in question, they can make recommendations on how to augment or diminish the force of each of the Five Elements in order to attain balance and flow, as well as to address particular issues in the lives of the occupants.

To use the Feng Shui Kitchen Ba Gua to analyze a space—a room or an entire house—align the directions on the octagon with the actual compass directions from where you stand. For instance, the Fire side, or gua, should be pointing toward the south, and Water should point north. Now imagine the octagon as the room or house, and read which characteristics and properties are associated with each area. Your south wall, for instance, is the home of Fire, or fame and rank, and you can activate these energies by adding red accents or placing a stove, fireplace, or candle there. Check the east sector of your room or house if you've been having health problems. Is it dirty or cluttered? Clean it up and add a green plant to please Wood, whose powers can heal and mend.

The Ba Gua and Your Food

Likewise, the Feng Shui Kitchen Ba Gua can help you choose your food and arrange it on the plate to maximize its elemental powers.

In Chinese medicine and psychology, each person is thought to possess a unique combination of the Five Elements, usually with a dominant one that shapes your personality and physiology. The best health and success, however, come from a harmonious balance among the five.

Foods are associated with the Five Elements through their colors and flavors, as depicted by the Feng Shui Kitchen Ba Gua. If you're deficient in one or more elements, either temporarily or characteristically, you can balance your energy by eating foods with those elements' flavors and colors. You'll learn more about the elemental properties of food and eating for yin-yang balance in the Chapter "Feng Shui Food."

To apply the Feng Shui Kitchen Ba Gua to your plate, align Fire with the top, Water with the bottom, and arrange your food so that the flavors and colors reinforce the elements of each gua. Each recipe in this book provides serving instructions for creating a feng shui plate that activates the energies you seek—and creates a colorful presentation to make your meal as beautiful as it is delicious.

The Ba Gua in Your Life

The Feng Shui Kitchen Ba Gua is a quick reference to feng shui principles that can help you arrange your space and plan your meals. Its visual portrayal of life situations can also serve as a basis for self-assessment, meditation, and discovery. Have you been favoring career over health? Family over knowledge? Reflecting upon the guas can help you ask questions, juggle priorities, and remember values.

Make a photocopy of the Feng Shui Kitchen Ba Gua and post it on your refrigerator door or another convenient spot. A glance will remind you which flavors and colors can help you achieve your current energy goals as you cook; provide a visual cue for maximizing the qi of your environment and your plate; and offer a concise image of multidimensional priorities and issues working together in a unified whole. The ba gua is the picture of a balanced life.

WHY FENG SHUI YOUR FOOD?

China had imperial nutritionists as early as the fourth century B.C. The *Yellow Emperor's Manual* described diabetes in detail and linked its incidence to dietary habits. BY A.D. 200, doctors were aware of dietary deficiency diseases, as noted in Chang Chi's *Systematic Treasury of Medicine*. Hu Ssu-Hui's *Principles of Correct Diet*, published in 1330, stated that "Many diseases can be cured by diet alone." Today, Chinese doctors generally look at diet as the first line of treatment for disease, turning to other methods only after food's healing potential has been fully exploited.

The Chinese tradition was light-years ahead of Western culture, in which deficiency and diet-related diseases were only recognized centuries later. American nutrition developed as a science at the turn of the twentieth century with the misguided notion that the healthiest diet maximized protein and fat! The U.S. government only managed to overcome the agribusiness lobby and mobilize scientific resources to issue nutritional guidelines as recently as the 1970s, and most Americans currently opt for restaurants, take-out, or packaged foods when it's time to replenish essential energy. No wonder we persistently behave like babes in the woods about how to cook and eat—and no wonder China enjoys a lower rate of diet- and lifestyle-related diseases than we do.

In China, the I Ching and its theory of yin-yang balance came to the fore as an antidote to the turmoil of the Warring States period (circa 500 to 200 B.C.). As people sought a sense of connection to their environment and centeredness in themselves to guide them

through the chaos, the principle of balanced energies became not just a temporary solace but an enduring wisdom that has sustained and nurtured Chinese civilization for over two thousand years.

Today, in the West, as technology reinvents our reality on a daily basis, livelihoods are downsized without warning, and conflicting nutritional theories and fads lead to confusion at best and illness, even death, at worst, you could say that we live in our own period of Warring States. Like the people of that time, we need to reconnect with a sense of our vital life force.

The Feng Shui Cookbook will give you the tools you need to find this life force in your daily diet. It will help you assess both your basic nature and your yin-yang balance at any given time, and then to eat the delicious food that will maximize your qi and adjust for any energy imbalances. You'll sit down to cool Gingered Sweet Potato Soup when you're stressed . . . and warm up with Fire-Roasted Filet Mignon when you need motivation and peak performance. You can fight burnout with the yin energy of Banana Coconut Cream Pudding or feed your creative fire with Drunken Firepot Shrimp. And you can experience and internalize balance with the perfect harmony of dishes such as Five-Element Peanut Noodles or a Flexible Stir-Fry.

Perhaps it's time for you to break free from rigid eating habits that limit your nutritional and sensual horizons. Maybe your own low energy levels are telling you to get rid of the boil-in-the-bag and remember what food looked, tasted, and felt like before technology denatured it of its vitality. Or maybe, like most people, you wish you could have more energy and less stress, match your input with your output, prepare for and adjust to life's challenges and changes, and give yourself what you truly need now.

When you eat according to the everyday flow of yin and yang energy—the changing need to act or reflect, assert or accept, create or receive, speed up or slow down—you achieve harmony between external demands and your own inner needs. This rebalancing act promotes energy, health, success—qi.

Using *The Feng Shui Cookbook* can immediately increase your prosperity simply by cutting down on your food bills. Home cooking from real ingredients is generally more economical than buying prepared or packaged foods and is far cheaper than relying on take-out and restaurant meals. And soon you might find yourself spending less time and money at the doctor, the drugstore, or the vitamin counter. Chinese medical practitioners agree that junk food weakens qi, but real food that balances your constitution and your current life dynamics strengthens it, preventing disease and the need for piecemeal treatments of the symptoms of imbalance. This vital energy empowers you to attain ever-greater success in all of your ventures.

Whether you're entertaining, feeding the family, or dining alone, *The Feng Shui Cookbook*'s marriage of ancient wisdom with fresh food can add good taste and soul to all your meals. The simple act of making time to cook and nourish yourself with nature's miraculous bounty will make you more mindful and appreciative of the process of living. Pay heed to what you seek to fill your mouth with . . . and good fortune will be yours.

The Enlightened Eating Environment

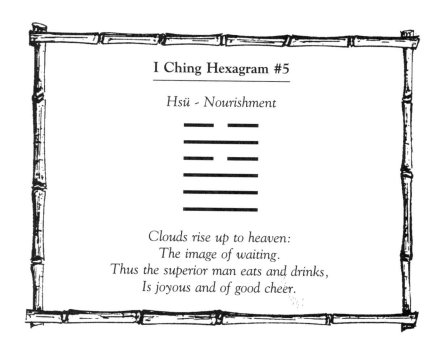

I Ching Hexagram #5

Hsü - Nourishment

Clouds rise up to heaven:
The image of waiting.
Thus the superior man eats and drinks,
Is joyous and of good cheer.

Feng shui holds that the most important rooms of the house are the bedroom, where you spend about a third of your life, and the kitchen, where the preparation of food determines the health—and hence the wealth—of all the house's occupants.

In your home, good feng shui translates into light, ventilation, proportion, and a sense of balance. By applying these principles to your kitchen and dining room, you can ensure that good qi surrounds and infuses your cooking and eating, enabling you to make every meal peaceful and energizing. As you bring these rooms into balance, you might find yourself less drawn to fast-food joints, and happier being in the heart of your very own home.

GET ORIENTED

Do you think about eating more than you'd like to? Maybe it's because you can see your kitchen when you walk in your front door, which feng shui says can lead to a chronic problem of food on the brain. This can also extend to your guests, who could take to dropping by hungry a bit more often than you'd like. Break this visual-psychological loop by closing the kitchen door or placing a screen to conceal its entry from the front hall.

If, on the other hand, your kitchen's interior seems as alien to you as the moon—if you find yourself settling for a steady diet of pepperoni at the corner pizzeria rather than venturing into this strange and forbidding space—perhaps your kitchen doesn't really "belong" to the house. Rooms that sit in front of the main entryway—for example, in the wings of a U-shaped structure with the front door at the concave part—feel like they're outside the house rather than part of it, and thus discourage you from spending time there. If your kitchen or dining room suffers from this misalignment, you might be disinclined to dine in. The feng shui solution is to build a gated fence connecting the top of the U, to create a front courtyard that will reintegrate these rooms into your house and prevent the unconscious habit of eating out. Too many restaurants can squander your money and potentially your health, as well as deprive you of the joyful and self-nurturing process of cooking your own food.

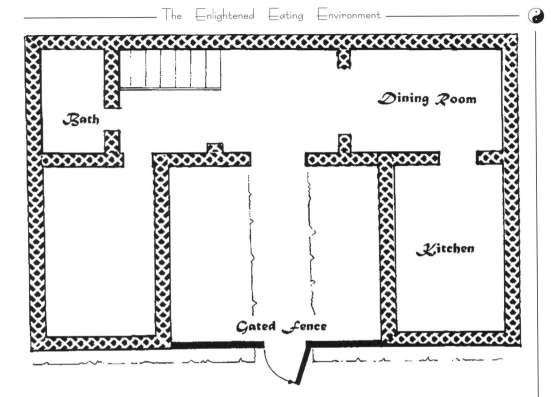

The very best placement for the kitchen is on the east side of the house, where you can greet the morning sun with your breakfast and prepare the evening meal without glare in your eyes. It's best to avoid the northeast and southwest corners of the house, as these are considered doors of the devil and no place to be preparing food. North and northwest are also not favored. If you're adding onto your kitchen and creating a projection beyond the lines of the house, the northwest and southeast corners are the most promising.

The kitchen and dining room should be as close to each other as possible—which, in addition to being auspicious, makes serving and cleanup easier—and both should be placed well away from any bathrooms, where the abundance represented by food can be flushed away.

THE KITCHEN

The Hot Spot

Within the kitchen, feng shui considers the stove the most important place. A symbol of good fortune, your stove provides the transformational fire that turns raw ingredients into cooked food, and so represents the human potential realized when the first cave person harnessed the power of fire. It's best if you can put the stove on a south wall—the home of its element, Fire—but in no case should it be placed in a dead corner without the light and ventilation that circulate qi and keep the cook comfortable.

Avoid placing the stove next to the sink or refrigerator, which causes a conflict between the opposing elements of Fire and Water, while the heat of the stove makes your refrigerator work harder and drives up your utility bills. And make sure that the cook can see the kitchen door while standing at the stove so as not to be startled by others who enter the room. A nervous cook can ruin the meal and thus the harmony of the entire household. If you have no choice but to cook with your back to the kitchen door, hang a mirror or well-polished wok or pan over the stove to enable you to keep an eye out. This reflection also symbolically doubles the quantity of food being cooked, connoting wealth and abundance.

Other feng shui guidelines for maximizing the qi of the all-important stove include a powerful updraft ventilation system, unimpeded by any low-hanging cupboards or microwave ovens. The best cooktop is powered by gas, producing real Fire instead of its denatured electrical analogue, and making it easier to regulate the temperature as you cook, which is key to good and consistent results. You should rotate your use of burners to keep good fortune flowing—and prevent too much wear and tear on any single one. A cutting board made of Wood next to the stove provides Fire with perpetual fuel, and makes an easy transition from knife to pan. And don't forget to hang a Kitchen God above the stove to keep you connected with the heavens.

The Kitchen God: Heaven's Eyes and Ears

It's no accident that the Chinese god in charge of all household matters resides in the kitchen, the heart of the home. In fact, the Kitchen God prefers to be hung, in wooden or paper form, above the stove—the spot where the very qi of the family originates, and an excellent vantage point from which to observe your goings-on. You can buy a Kitchen God for your stove at Chinese import stores, or make a copy of this drawing (the deity might appreciate an enlargement along the way).

The Kitchen God makes an annual report to the heavens on the family's good deeds and transgressions, so it's a good idea to smear honey on his lips each New Year (the twenty-third day of the twelfth month of the lunar calendar) to ensure that his words will be sweet. And be advised: The Kitchen God is especially attuned to romantic misdeeds—so by all means keep your indiscretions out of the kitchen.

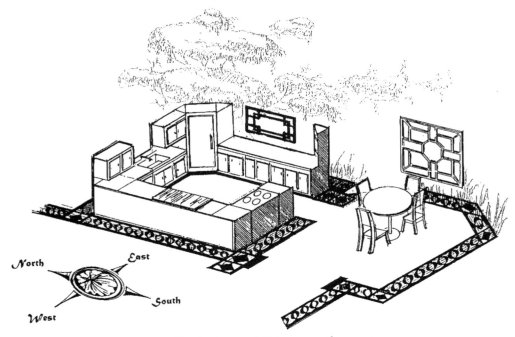

North
East
South
West

Feng Shui kitchen and dining room placement

Water and the Flow of Wealth

Water has been associated with prosperity since the Chinese became the world's first rice farmers, staking their very sustenance upon one of the thirstiest crops on the planet. Food means wealth, and rice needs water, so an ample and free-flowing water supply connotes good fortune in feng shui theory.

For this reason, you should keep your kitchen sink—your home's most important source of water—clean and in good working order. That means no clogged drains, missing washers, or strainers filled with debris. Don't let your faucets leak; the constant drip can wash your money away, most directly in the form of higher utility bills. A north wall, where Water resides in the ba gua, is a good place for the sink.

Light

The best light is natural, so the optimal feng shui kitchen has windows that light the stove, sink, and countertops. Glare, however, creates unfavorable sha qi, so if you have a west-ward-facing window, which admits glare in the late afternoon when you're likely to be preparing dinner, position the sink, stove, and chopping blocks so you don't have to face it, or install a good blind that admits soft, filtered light.

For your artificial lighting, avoid the glare of fluorescent fixtures and exposed bulbs, whose excess yang energy can be exacerbated by reflective white walls, and opt instead for a soft but powerful source, such as track lighting.

Colors

White is the color of purity and cleanliness, and feng shui favors it for your kitchen walls. White is also the color of Metal, which submits to Fire in the cycle of the Five Elements, allowing the stove's power to prevail in this room. By making white your basic color choice for the kitchen, you create a canvas against which the colorful ingredients of your cooking can shine.

Beware of too much red in the kitchen: Fire's color can combine with the heat of the stove to make a hot and bothered cook. Black, the color of Water, can also be counterproductive because it seeks to extinguish Fire and so impedes your cooking efforts. Both colors can be used as accents, though.

Angles and Edges

Sharp angles and corners are thought to speed and concentrate qi, aiming it like an arrow at anyone who stands in its path, with detrimental effect. In the kitchen, avoid any sharp

angles created by walls, furniture, or appliances that could point at you as you cook. If a protruding corner skewers you with bad qi while you stand at the stove, soften it with a mirror or plant. Rearrange furniture or appliances as necessary, and choose soft and rounded contours over sharp ones.

Exposed rafters or beams hanging over the stove could inhibit your financial opportunity as well as make you feel crowded and offer an unwanted opportunity to bump your head. Avoid claustrophobia with an overhead mirror, or alert your head to incipient danger by hanging a ribbon or chime.

Clutter

As the center of health, prosperity, and familial harmony, the kitchen should be clean and uncluttered at all times. Crowded circumstances impede the free flow of qi and make the cook mad, often at a subconscious level that can lead to frustration with the whole cooking enterprise.

To improve your kitchen's qi, clean out your refrigerator and cupboards, discarding old food and worn-out or damaged dishes, pots, pans, and appliances. Move special-occasion items to a storage area that doesn't experience heavy use. Clear off your countertops, finding permanent homes for the items that congregate there.

When it's time to cook, finding inspiration and guidance should be fun, not a source of irritation and stress, so good recipe organization is essential. Consider a bookshelf in the kitchen for your cookbooks. Keep clipped recipes in an accordion file and review them every year; throw away anything you haven't tried, or tried and didn't like.

Your kitchen should reflect a sense of space, order, and peace so that the food you prepare there will convey those qualities to the people who eat it. An annual kitchen cleaning before the Kitchen God's New Year report to the heavens can help keep your celestial balance sheet clean, and restore your joy in the daily process of nourishing yourself and your loved ones.

Applying the Feng Shui Kitchen Ba Gua

Would you like your partner to be more involved in the kitchen? Consult the Feng Shui Kitchen Ba Gua and you'll see that the southwest corner is the partnership area of the room, and you can activate its energy by decorating it in red, pink, or white. Or perhaps you'd like to solicit more help from family or friends: Try accents of white, gray, or black in the helpful people gua to the northwest.

To fine-tune your kitchen's qi to your needs, use the Feng Shui Kitchen Ba Gua to determine the orientation of the qualities you seek, and enhance that part of the room with the appropriate colors or elements. Every kitchen, for instance, should have a green plant in the east, where Wood and the energy of family and health reside. You're also applying the Feng Shui Kitchen Ba Gua when you position your stove in Fire's southern gua, or place the sink in Water's northern gua to maximize your cash flow.

THE DINING ROOM

Seating

Would you rather dine in heaven or on earth? A round dining table signifies heaven—and facilitates the sharing of food and conversation—while a square table's association with earth makes it a less inspiring shape. The table should be in the center of the room with good lighting and ventilation to ensure the flow of qi.

Chairs should number four, six, or eight. Even numbers represent luck, but an odd one implies loneliness. Empty chairs can make you miss absent friends or relatives, so put away any unoccupied seats. Arrange the chairs so that nobody sits with his or her back to the door, or faces a close corner or wall.

Light

As in the kitchen, it's desirable to have as much natural light in the dining room as the seasonal schedule of sun allows. A windowed wall is ideal for letting in light. Add a mirror to the wall opposite the windows to draw in good qi and reflect it onto the table, doubling and blessing your food. Be sure this mirror doesn't cut off the top of any diner's head; the negative implications are obvious.

Candles can enhance any evening meal. If you're emphasizing yin energy for relaxation, just a few well-shielded ones will do. But if you'd rather stimulate yang, try clusters of candles arranged on reflective platters or mirrors.

Colors

In the dining room, use red for good luck, gold for fortune, and plants to encourage qi to grow. Many Chinese restaurants install fish tanks in the dining room because both water and the fish that swim in it symbolize wealth. On the other hand, fish in water are also a Chinese metaphor for sexual pleasure, so come to your own conclusion about fish tanks in the dining room.

You can decorate the table to reinforce the elemental colors of the food you're eating, or to represent the full feng shui palette of green, red, yellow, white, and black. Use tablecloths, napkins, plates, flowers, candles, and centerpieces to play up the colors that serve your current needs. For instance, you might want to avoid a lot of red, the color of Fire, when you're trying to unwind after a stressful day; instead, emphasize the Earth color of yellow (also golds and browns). Save your red tablecloth to stimulate a lively party or celebrate a fortunate event.

You'll learn more about the different properties of the Five Elements and their colors in "Feng Shui Food."

A Few More Details

Exposed rafters or beams over the dining room table are undesirable. Who wants to think of the weight of the world—or at least the house—while they dine? If possible, position the table so it's free of such oppressive forces; otherwise, an overhead mirror can lighten the load. Likewise, avoid sharp corners that will shoot arrows of bad qi at diners while they eat.

To bestow blessings, good luck, and the promise of new opportunity upon your meals, scatter barley or wheat in the kitchen and dining room, using an upward toss. This can be a good cleanser after a meal has gone awry—something burned, a diner taken ill, or an unfortunate interpersonal incident.

You can help make your meals a source of family togetherness and well-being by placing a plant on an east wall to activate Wood, the element of family and health. And remember that the dining room is no place for papers, books, appliances, or other qi-blocking clutter. More than any other room of the house, the dining room's atmosphere should be one of peace and beauty.

ENLIGHTENED EATING

To ensure the best qi in your cooking and eating environment, make your own assessment of your kitchen and dining room. How do they make you feel?

When you set out to cook, is it with a sense of adventure and anticipation, or do you feel irritated that there aren't enough hours in the day and it takes five minutes to get out a skillet because it's in an inconvenient cupboard with other things stacked on top? The feng shui kitchen should ease the cooking process, unleash your creativity, and make you feel deeply at home.

Sit down where you usually eat. What do you see from there? Stacks of unpaid bills on the mail table? The kids' clutter in the family room? Rearrange the room and table so you look out the window at a nice view, at a beautiful piece of art, or into another, well-kept room that pleases you.

If you find your kitchen attracting family members and guests, then you've achieved good feng shui there. If your dining room encourages you to eat slowly, peacefully, and joyfully, then you've established the right flow of environmental qi. And now you're ready to eat for essential energy.

Feng Shui Food

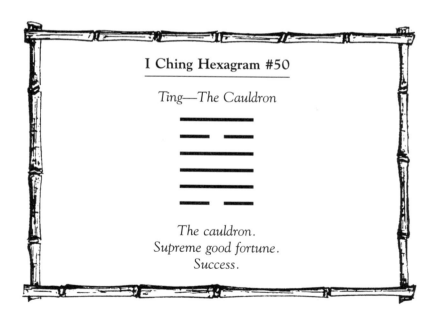

I Ching Hexagram #50

Ting—The Cauldron

The cauldron.
Supreme good fortune.
Success.

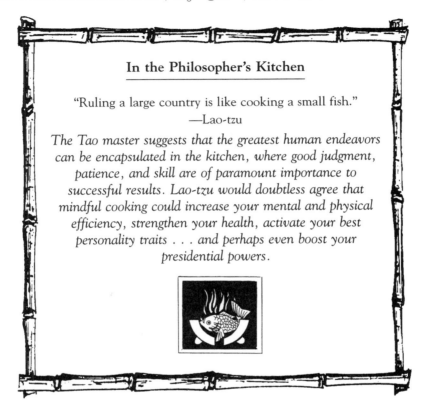

In the Philosopher's Kitchen

"Ruling a large country is like cooking a small fish."
—Lao-tzu

The Tao master suggests that the greatest human endeavors can be encapsulated in the kitchen, where good judgment, patience, and skill are of paramount importance to successful results. Lao-tzu would doubtless agree that mindful cooking could increase your mental and physical efficiency, strengthen your health, activate your best personality traits . . . and perhaps even boost your presidential powers.

Many feng shui masters call their practice a cross between a science and an art. So do a lot of cooks.

Feng shui's purpose is to tap the resources and powers of the earth, one of which is food. In simple biological terms, food is physical energy. But just as there are qualitative differences within energy levels—you can feel active or jittery, calm or fatigued—so the essential nature of the various foods you eat can create different kinds of qi. By harnessing and channeling the energies of food like feng shui masters do the forces of wind and water, you can rebalance your mind and body and achieve peak essential energy with every meal you eat.

YIN AND YANG

Yin and yang are the oppositional balancing forces that drive feng shui, the I Ching, and all of traditional Chinese philosophy. The interrelation and mutual dependence of dark yin and light yang are represented in the classic symbol pictured here.

Yang energy encompasses everything hard, strong, assertive, initiating, male. Images of bright fire, sun, the exterior, and the upper demonstrate how powerful and expanding yang energy is. Yang makes all the strength and power of heaven available to your initiative and progress. It helps you to lead, act, impel, move. To realize yang is *to do*.

Yin is the balancing principle to yang. Yin represents water, moon, lower, inner, female, dark, soft, moist. It's the earth below heaven, darkness illuminated by light, open space, an ear filled with talk. Yin energy provides fertile ground for the initiative impulses of the universe. It enables you to assist, follow, complete, listen; to renounce agendas and receive answers. Yin spreads your nurture like money, so power will come to your open arms. To realize yin is *to be*.

Based on the idea that the universe is dualistic by nature, feng shui finds that yin and yang resonate together. When yin meets yin or yang meets yang or either type of energy dominates, clashes and conflicts can arise.

Chinese medicine holds that you can balance your yin-yang energy with the food you eat. When you have too much watery yin energy—when you're cool, damp, or depleted—yang foods can warm you up and get you back to speed. If you're warm, dry, or congested, which indicates excess fiery yang energy, yin foods can cool you down and help you relax. The first step is to assess your own personal balance of yin-yang energy. Then you'll find out which foods you need to rebalance.

Yin and Yang: Opposites Attract

Yin is:	Yang is:
Subordinate	Superior
Feminine	Masculine
Water	Fire
Moon	Sun
Dark	Bright
Soft	Hard
Cool	Hot
Moist	Dry
Lower, inner	Upper, outer
Yielding, submissive, reactive, receptive, responsive, open, following	Strong, assertive, authoritative, initiating, manifest, expanding, moving
To be	To do

The Yin-Yang Self-Assessment

These checklists (see pages 32–33) assess the personality, physical, and emotional characteristics that determine the yin-yang balance of your qi. Check each item that pertains to you, then add up your check marks in each box. Circle the higher score from each yin-yang pair (cool-warm, damp-dry, and depleted-congested). The result is your three-dimensional yin-yang profile. Now add your scores horizontally to find out whether yin or yang dominates your qi.

You can take the test in two different ways, assessing:

Your Constitution   Answer the questions according to *the way you usually feel*. This is your essential, underlying yin-yang balance, which can help guide your food choices in general.

Your Current Energy Balance   Answer the questions according to *how you feel right now*. These results measure your current response to the ongoing change in your life, to help you choose your menu today. Stress can warm you up, while stagnation in your life could lead to symptoms of congestion. The flu is likely to make you warm and dry, but a bout of depression can cause you to feel cool and depleted. Summer makes most people hotter and drier, and winter brings on dampness and chills. When you're mad at someone, have a tension headache, or have been sitting in the sun too long, you've got too much yang. Lack of energy, ideas, or motivation indicate an excess of yin.

Note that while yin is associated with feminine attributes and yang with masculine, these are archetypal concepts unrelated to your actual gender. A man can be or feel yin, and a woman can burst with yang energy. Feng shui recommends balance between the two no matter what your sex!

Photocopy this test so that you can reassess your current energy balance any time you like.

Yin, Yang, and Food

You'll probably agree that certain foods have different types of energy. Red meat and red wine, for instance, seem hot, strong, masculine—yang. You'll find these ingredients in the yang dish Fire-Roasted Filet Mignon With Wild Mushroom Sauce. Yang foods such as these are thought to create inner warmth and stimulate circulation.

Soft, yielding foods, on the other hand, seem cool, feminine, domesticated—yin. Think juicy fruits and vegetables, milk, eggs, tofu. Yin foods cool you down.

Depending on your energy needs and goals, you can choose yin foods, yang foods, or a harmonious balance of both, such as a stir-fry of yang meat, yin vegetables, and neutral rice.

You probably know the feeling of well-being that follows a meal that's just right for your current state of mind and body. It tasted wonderful, feels just right in your stomach, and has left you satisfied and energized. If you experience this feeling occasionally but not often, you might not be matching the food you eat with your own variable states of energy. The *Feng Shui Cookbook* recipes are organized by yin, yang, or balanced effects to help you correct any imbalances you find in your yin-yang assessment and match the quality of your energy to the needs of your day or night.

Just as yin and yang are opposing forces that keep the world in balance, so the *Feng Shui Cookbook* recipes are based on a principle of balance that makes no food forbidden. While a deficit of yang may call for the richness of steak or a dark chocolate dessert, you can adjust for too little yin with the purity of Chilled Tofu With Scallions and Sesame Oil or Rice Stick Noodle Salad. The recipes draw on the whole range of ingredients that nature provides to rise above the confusion about "right" and "wrong" foods, instead celebrating equilibrium and the holistic nourishment of mind, body, and spirit.

In fact, the Chinese are one of few cultures that hold no particular food taboos. While religious Jews forbid pork, Muslims wine and pork, and Hindus beef—and most Westerners look with horror at a dish of horse, snake, or ducks' feet—the Chinese happily eat everything. This inherent joy of eating and belief in the benefits of all nature's bounty might lie at the heart of the good nutritional health characteristic of Chinese culture.

Likewise, the Chinese have attained excellent dietary balance without the counting of fat grams or parsing out of nutritional numbers that we (unsuccessfully) rely upon in the West. In fact, the Chinese holistic approach to health is quite the reverse. Rather than breaking foods down into numbers that fail to represent energy, essence, flavor—all the things that constitute their nourishing power—the emphasis is on being sensitive to hunger and maintaining balance at the whole-foods level. The word *diet*, in the sense of a weight-loss regime, doesn't even exist in the Chinese language. Instead, the philosophy is that if you eat a wide variety of foods, following the principles of balance and contrast, you will naturally feed your qi and maintain good health. The low obesity rate in China suggests that this works—especially when you follow the traditional dictum that you should stop eating before you're completely full, so that you always leave some room in your stomach for qi.

It's probably no coincidence that in the United States, our national obesity rate and calories consumed per capita have both increased since nutritional data became available on everything from bottled water to chocolate. *The Feng Shui Cookbook* suggests that you leave these mealtime mathematics behind, eat for your energy needs, leave a little empty room in your stomach to accommodate your qi, and enjoy the natural vitality of a fit body and mind.

Yin-Yang Self-Assessment—YIN

Cool	*Damp*	*Depleted*
___ Easily chilled or cold right now	___ Feel lethargic and heavy in general or today	___ Fatigue, chronic or today
___ Low blood pressure, slow metabolism, or poor circulation	___ Dislike humid environments, or feel damp now	___ Emotionally sensitive, in general or today
___ Adaptive to events and other people's opinions, or feeling so today	___ Skin and hair feel oily or clammy	___ Upset by noise
___ Physically calm, not fidgety, either now or in general	___ Not thirsty, either now or in general	___ Feel unmotivated or depressed, in general or today
___ Crave spicy and hot food and beveratges	___ Crave dry foods	___ Crave tart or rich food and beverages
Total (0–5)_____	Total (0–5)_____	Total (0–5)_____

Yin-Yang Self-Assessment—YANG

Warm	Dry	Congested
___ Uncomfortable in the heat, or hot right now	___ Dry skin, hair, or mouth in general or right now	___ Restlessness
___ Active and lively in general, or extra energy today	___ Uncomfortable in the wind or dry weather	___ Stress, feelings of internal pressure
___ Strong opinions and confidence	___ Easily irritated, or irritable today	___ Difficult digestion, constipation, or gas— chronic or now
___ Quick tempered, either now or in general	___ Thirsty, either now or in general	___ Nervousness or insomnia, in general or today
___ Crave cold food and beverages	___ Crave tart, juicy, or oily foods	___ Crave simple foods and beverages
Total (0–5)_____	Total (0–5)_____	Total (0–5)_____

Your **Yin** total (Cool + Damp + Depleted, 0–15) =_____
Your **Yang** total (Warm + Dry + Congested, 0–15) =_____
Scores are for (check one) **Constitution_____ Current Energy Balance_____**

Food's Essential Nature

The table (on page 35) shows some examples of the essential yin and yang energies of certain foods.

More generally, you can assess the yin-yang nature of foods by their category and method of preparation (see the table "The Essential Nature of Food: Coolest to Warmest" on page 36).

Because the yin or yang nature of food is relative to the person who eats it and to other foods, and is also affected by color and preparation method, this model is highly interactive. For instance, crab and chicken are considered cool even though poultry and seafood are generally warm. It also seems intuitively correct that delicate, white-fleshed sole is cooler than dark, oily tuna, and that steak is warmer than chicken. Hot soup is considered cooling because of all the yin water it contains; sushi is yin because it's eaten raw, but cooked fish is often yang. Vegetables are generally yin, but broccoli, because it's the male part of the plant, has more yang energy than female eggplant or tomatoes. Although a yam is neutral in nature, its orange color is associated with Earth and yin energy. But if you're cold, eating that yam broiled with some butter and ground ginger could warm you up significantly.

The relativity of yin and yang is illustrated by a feng shui analogy. The roof of a house is yang (above) relative to the ground, but yin (below) in relation to the heavens.

In this view, balance never lies in one place. There is no single food or combination of foods that promises good qi. Rather, as you nourish your life force through the act of cooking and eating, you strike multiple points of balance that harmonize the dynamics of your inner life, your external circumstances, and the moment.

Purposeful Imbalance

Sometimes balance is not your immediate goal. When you need extra assertiveness for an important presentation or deal, the time is right to muster all the yang energy at your command. Or maybe you want to become very calm and quiet to recover from a stressful day, or to meditate. Then you should become as yin as you can.

For specific goals such as these, look at the list of yin and yang attributes on page 29, decide which group of characteristics you seek right now, and choose recipes from that category. For instance, try:

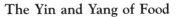

The Yin and Yang of Food

Yang (Warm–Hot)	Neutral	Yin (Cool–Cold)
Red meats	Pork	Crab
Alcohol and wine	Milk	Chicken
Coffee	Sweet potatoes	Cucumbers
Chocolate	Peanuts	Sesame seeds
Ginger	Rice	Seaweed
Butter	Figs	Water or broth
Shrimp	Carrots	Apples
Walnuts	Honey	Oranges
Chilies		Mangoes
Cinnamon, cloves,		Ice cream, frozen yogurt
nutmeg, pepper,		
and most spices		

- A yin lunch like Rice Stick Noodle Salad to fight stress.
- A yang lunch like Quick Chickpea Curry to gear up for a productive afternoon.
- A yin dinner like Grapefruit-Poached Sole With Watercress Sauce to relax after a busy day.
- A yang dinner like Chili-Honey Barbecued Baby Back Ribs to restart your engine after too long at your desk.

Once your goals are accomplished, Chinese medicine recommends that you return to a balanced condition to protect against the stress of prolonged excess.

The Essential Nature of Food: Coolest to Warmest

Food Type	Preparation Method
COOLEST	COOLEST
↓ Soft, juicy fruits	↓ Raw, fresh
↓ Crisper, harder fruits	↓ Raw, dried
↓ Nonroot vegetables	↓ Steamed
↓ Root vegetables	↓ Sautéed
↓ Grains	↓ Baked
↓ Seeds	↓ Fried
↓ Nuts	↓ Roasted
↓ Legumes	↓ Broiled or grilled
↓ Milk, cheese, eggs	WARMEST
↓ Seafood, poultry, meat	
WARMEST	

Another way to use the yin and yang properties of foods to achieve natural good health and qi is to keep a running balance. If you ate yang for lunch, keep dinner on the yin side. A week of yin eating habits—salads and simple, cool things—might leave you craving yang; go right ahead and have that steak, or something spicy or fried. Create balanced meals by combining a yin dish with a yang one, or enjoy the recipes noted as balanced.

FOOD AND THE FIVE ELEMENTS

If yin and yang are the parents of feng shui and Chinese medicine, the Five Elements are their aunts and uncles. Each of the Five Elements—Wood, Fire, Earth, Metal, and Water—arises from the interplay of yin and yang, and has particular characteristics and powers. In

Balancing the Energy Equation

Yang: Gear Up	*Yin: Chill Out*

- Choose meat or shrimp instead of chicken or fish, or chicken or fish instead of a vegetarian meal, or grains and potatoes instead of just vegetables.

- Spice things up with chilies, fresh ginger, pepper, rosemary, basil, or dried spices such as ginger, nutmeg, or ground ginger.

- Start your day with an omelette, a compote of gingered peaches and raspberries, and a cup of coffee.

- Clear your head with a cup of Fresh Ginger Tea or ginseng tea.

- Add a sprinkle of sunflower seeds or walnuts (which are thought to boost your brain power) to whatever you're eating.

- Choose chicken or seafood instead of meat, or grains or potatoes instead of chicken or seafood . . . or, better yet, have soup and salad.

- Take a break with a wedge of cool watermelon or an orange.

- Brew a cup of green tea. Stop and do nothing while you drink it.

- Treat yourself to a frozen yogurt.

- Toss together a moisturizing salad of bamboo shoots, water chestnuts, and cucumbers.

- Steer clear of fried or spicy foods, coffee, chocolate, and alcohol.

THE FIVE ELEMENTS

Traits	Personality Proportions	Emotion	Body and Qi	Dynamic
WOOD (Sour/Green)				
Benevolence, loyalty, forgiveness.	*Balanced:* Attentive, reflective; you make your own decisions. *Excess:* Inflexible and prejudiced. *Deficient:* Wishy-washy.	Anger.	Cleansing, gathering, concentrates qi; tones nerves; good for the liver. *Excess* causes cramping and pain.	Family and health. Active and growing, spring, daybreak
FIRE (Bitter/Red)				
Wisdom, reason, etiquette.	*Balanced:* Assertive; your anger is justified by principle and logic. *Excess:* Quick-tempered, loud, unreasonable, critical. *Deficient:* Self-pitying, weak, unassertive.	Joy.	Drying, strengthening, detoxifying; discharges qi downward; good for heart and blood. *Excess* dissipates qi and moisture.	Fame and rank. Maximum productivity, summer, noon.
EARTH (Sweet-bland/Yellow-orange, brown)				
Honesty, faith.	*Balanced:* Honest, dependable, helpful. *Excess:* Old-fashioned, rigid, self sacrificing. *Deficient:* Cheap, selfish, procrastinating, opportunistic.	Wonder, meditation.	Harmonizing, nourishing, expanding, relaxing, moisturizing; supplements qi and slows it down; good for the spleen. *Excess* produces congestion and heat.	Yin-yang balance, transition.

Traits	Personality Proportion	Emotion	Body and Qi	Dynamic
		METAL (Hot-spicy/White)		
Righteousness.	*Balanced:* Independent, principled, able to criticize wrong without excess. *Excess:* Self-righteous, gossipy, critical, argumentative, complaining. *Deficient:* Overly careful, appearing aloof and arrogant.	Sadness, depression.	Stimulating, dispersing; accelerates the circulation of qi and blood; relieves stagnation; good for the lungs. *Excess* exhausts qi and blood.	Children. Relaxing or recovering, autumn, sunset.
		WATER (Salty/Black)		
Moving—motivation and social contacts. Still—clarity of mind.	*Balanced:* Moving—powerful, directed, and well connected; still—innate understanding. *Excess:* Moving—unpredictable but attractive; still—pure knowledge and essential intuition. *Deficient:* Moving—shy, homebound; still—limited vision, stuck in a rut.	Fear.	Softening, densifying, concentrating; dissolves congealed qi; supplements blood and essence; good for the kidneys. *Excess* congeals blood and essence.	Career. Maximum repose, winter, midnight.

Chinese Nutritional Medicine

The practice of Chinese nutritional medicine is as complex as it is ancient. Based on yin and yang, the Five Elements, and various parameters of dysfunction in the body, nutritional therapy is a central part of traditional Chinese medicine, and it requires personal consultation with a trained doctor to implement the full nuances of the system.

In addition to optimizing health through the properties of everyday foods, Chinese nutritional medicine also relies on herbs, which can be taken in pills, infused in teas, or cooked into food. At the Snake King restaurant in Hong Kong, for instance, diners can order up medicinal soups made of venomous snakes if they like, or chicken with fresh water chestnuts, or a soup of turtle and chicken feet reputed to be good for the yin—all with the right herbs to cure whatever ails you. There's an entire pharmacology of healing herbal soups designed to supplement and harmonize, decongest, dry out, moisten, and warm up each of the Five Elements. For most people, these are an acquired taste.

Recipes for such herbal medications were cataloged in China as early as the sixteenth century A.D., when Li Shi-jen came up with over twelve thousand formulations. Today, sales of herbal supplements in the United States are soaring, and experts agree that herbs can be an effective treatment for conditions such as colds and flu, short-term memory loss, insomnia, migraine, and digestive distress. For more on Chinese medicine and herbology, see "Recommended Reading" on page 219.

fact, the Five Elements are essentially how the Chinese explain the differences among things, situations, seasons, emotions, and people. Each person is considered to possess various proportions of the elements, with one generally dominating. And you can manipulate your elemental balance through food.

In cooking, the powers of the Five Elements are activated by foods of their associated color, and by the correlate Five Flavors: sweet, sour, salty, bitter, and hot. Harmony and balance among these flavors are the marks of a good recipe, and considered necessary to good health. Each flavor's and color's link to a specific element gives it a certain power in the body and mind. If you have a sweet tooth, you'll be glad to learn that sweetness is a harmonizing force!

The table called "The Five Elements" on page 40 summarizes the effect of the Five Elements on your personality, your emotions, and your body, and what can happen when they get out of balance.

When you eat food associated with a particular element, you enact that element's energy on your mind, body, and qi. Such foods can also help you experience and express the emotions associated with each element. So whether you seek an essential trait, an attitude adjustment, a physical or emotional feeling, or a particular kind of energy, the foods of the Five Elements can fine-tune your diet to your needs.

In addition to the flavors and colors that call up the powers of the Five Elements, there's also a meat, grain, fruit, and vegetable associated with each one. Following is a reference list of recommended foods and recipes to access the energy of a particular element.

WOOD

Meat: chicken or poultry
Grain: wheat
Fruit: peach
Vegetable: mallow

Green or sour foods:
Broccoli with a squeeze
　of lime
Vinegar
Lemon
Lime
All green vegetables

Wood Recipes

Asparagus, Spinach, and Shiitake Salad With Miso Dressing
Grapefruit-Poached Sole With Watercress Sauce
Lime Pie
Mu Shu Chicken Wrap
Pork and Shrimp Wontons With Cilantro Pesto
Rice Stick Noodle Salad
Tamarind Cooler With Lime Cubes

FIRE

Meat: lamb
Grain: glutinous millet
Fruit: plum
Vegetable: coarse greens
Red or bitter foods:
Beets
Red peppers
Tomatoes
Shrimp, lobster

Mustard greens
Radish
Horseradish
Turnip
Cucumber
Arugula
Bitter melon
Radicchio
Red wine

Fire Recipes

Chicken and Daikon in Red Wine Sauce
Fire-Roasted Filet Mignon With Wild Mushroom Sauce
and Arugula Mashed Potatoes
Lively Lentil Salad
Peppered Tuna With Wasabi Sauce
Seared Salmon With Horseradish Butter

EARTH

Meat: beef
Grain: millet
Fruit: apricot
Vegetable: scallions
Yellow (orange, brown) or sweet foods:
Turmeric, curry
Sweet potatoes, yams

Winter squash
Carrots
Peanuts
Orange peel
Eggs
Honey
Sugar

Earth Recipes

Gingered Sweet Potato Soup
Pineapple-Ham-Stuffed Yam
Green Tea Tofu Flans
Lamb Satay With Peanut Sauce
Orange-Braised Tofu
Stuffed Butternut Squash

METAL

Meat: horse
Grain: rice
Fruit: chestnut
Vegetable: onion
White or spicy foods:
White rice
Soybeans, tofu
Turkey breast, chicken breast
White fish, shellfish
Egg whites
Chrysanthemum tea

White beans
Milk, cream, yogurt, sour cream
Napa cabbage
Bok choy (translates as "white vegetable")
Jicama
Chilies
Ginger
Peppercorns, Szechwan peppercorns
Mustard seeds

Metal Recipes

Chicken Soup for a Cold
Chili Oil
Crab and Cucumber Salad
Pacific Martinis
Spicy Sesame Chicken
White-Hot Cabbage Slaw

(Fortunately, many people love spicy food, as most of us aren't likely to get our dose of Metal from horse meat!)

WATER

Meat: pork
Grain: beans or peas
Fruit: date
Vegetable: leek
Black or salty foods:
Black beans
Fermented black bean sauce
Black pepper
Black olives
Squid ink pasta
Black mushrooms
Soy sauce
Fish sauce
Salt

Water Recipes

Black Bean–Stuffed Chicken Breast
Miso Soup
Sensuous Squab
Thai Tacos
Yin-Yang Salad

The *Feng Shui Cookbook* recipes describe the elemental properties of each dish to help you access their particular properties. For instance, try a dose of Water energy with Black Bean–Stuffed Chicken Breast when you seek social contacts or career advancement—or need to face the fear involved in pursuing them.

Using the Five Elements as a color palette for your cooking has a health advantage, too. In general, the more colorful your food is, the more nutrients it contains, and feng shui's elemental color scheme helps ensure that you eat nutrient-dense foods in a wide variety. An orange yam of Earth, the green spinach of Wood, some sweet red strawberries for Fire, Metal's white tofu, the black beans of Water—all of these superfoods keep you well and enhance your longevity as they activate elemental powers in the recipes.

The Five-Element Creative Cycle

In addition to their individual characteristics, the Five Elements work together in creative and destructive cycles that spring from the interaction of their properties.

Feng shui seeks to maximize productive energy between the elements by combining those that support each other in the creative cycle. For instance, Wood feeds Fire, Fire creates new Earth with the production of ash, Earth protects Metal in the form of ore beneath its crust, Metal creates Water through condensation, and Water nourishes Wood and makes it grow.

You'll find segments of the creative (also called productive) cycle in the *Feng Shui Cookbook* recipes, which add auspicious energy to the dish to better feed your qi.

MOVEMENT AND SEASONS

Food also *moves*—up, down, in, and out. An inward-sinking food such as lettuce will go to your center and nourish your inner organs. Outward-floating foods such as pepper move toward the body's surface and encourage you to sweat out impurities. Milk moves upward to energize the upper body, and apples descend to counter ascending problems such as coughing and asthma.

5 Element
Creative Cycle

Fire

Wood

Earth

Water

Metal

The yin or yang nature of foods combines with their direction of movement to determine their season, or the time of year when they'll benefit you the most. Your food can facilitate seasonal transitions to help you move from one to the next without the colds or energy imbalances that changes in weather can bring.

Spring heralds the time when your qi should start to move upward, like a germinating plant. **Oyster Egg Custard** features such upward-moving foods as eggs, oysters, carrots, and celery to nudge your energy skyward.

Summer requires up- and outward-moving, cool dishes to disperse your qi to the surface, eliminate toxins, and avoid summer sluggishness. **Green Grape Gazpacho** does the job with upward-moving grapes and outward-moving green pepper, dried ginger, and white pepper, cooled by the refrigerator and the yin of sour lime.

In *autumn* you want to draw your energy back down, like plowing a harvested field back under, with a dish such as warm, downward-moving **Mending Moussaka.** Lamb traditionally celebrates the first day of fall and is considered to be mending, while mushrooms and eggplant move your qi downward to brace you for the winter ahead.

The trials of *winter* are best met with inward-moving warm and hot foods. **Salt-Roasted Duck With Beer-Braised Cabbage** warms you with richness and spice, while inward-moving hops and salt concentrate your qi within to keep you fortified and warm through the earth's period of dormancy and rest. Fresh ginger adds protection against wind, dampness, and cold, and garlic is an antibacterial to fight the infections and illness that winter weather can bring.

You might also want to try **Chicken Soup for a Cold** when any change in weather nabs you with a virus.

CONSCIOUS COOKING

Feng shui pays ultimate respect to nature, seeking always to protect, never to deplete, the environment. Likewise, eating foods produced in accord with nature is an important step toward balancing your qi. Look for fresh, local, and organic ingredients that are environmentally friendly and contain no additives or preservatives. Avoid packaged and processed foods, which have been stripped of their qi, whenever you can. Once you experience the quick simplicity of a naturally fast food such as Chilled Tofu With Scallions and Sesame Oil, you might never return to the energy-impaired alternatives.

The Chinese character for *fresh* also means "flavorful" when used in the context of food. This equation of freshness with good taste is another benefit of the Chinese way of eating. Fresh foods are simply the most delicious.

Another linguistic fact reveals the Chinese worldview toward food: In China, a dish is evaluated on the basis of taste, fragrance, color, and an untranslatable term for a quality that enables you to taste the meaning behind the food. *The Feng Shui Cookbook* is intended to take you to that untranslatable place, where the right food can have a meaningful and positive impact on your life—as well as being beautiful, aromatic, and delicious!

The most important aspect of the feng shui kitchen is your own presence in the moment. Begin with five-sense cooking:

- **Look.** In addition to helping you read labels and work more safely with knives, your eyes can tell you how your dish is coming along. Many things shine when they're ready to move to the next stage—perfectly sautéed peppers, for instance, whose gloss says, "Look at me! I'm ready!"

- **Listen.** Food speaks. A fast, angry sizzle tells you the sauté is running dry. Sputters and pops from the broiler are your steaks asking to be turned.

- **Smell.** Most foods smell more like themselves when they're done cooking and ready to eat—garlic, mushrooms, tomatoes, meat.

- **Touch.** A gentle squeeze can tell you whether fruit is ripe or vegetables are fresh. Meat and fish become firm to the touch as they cook through; vegetables and starches soften. Many people consider the tactile sensation of handling food one of the greatest joys of cooking.

- **Taste.** Even the wisest recipe can't know as much as the taste buds on your tongue. Good cooks agree that tasting as you go is essential to success, so when in doubt, sample.

With your senses in gear, now move inward. Your perceptions of the process of cooking and eating can influence its effect on your qi, and a positive mind-set can enhance the mind-body nutritional value of your food. Do you view your time in the kitchen and at the table as important? Peaceful? Fun? Sensually pleasurable? Do you congratulate your aesthetic accomplishments and cherish the life-sustaining process of nourishing yourself and others? These are the kinds of thoughts and intentions that translate ingredients into food for your life force.

If, on the other hand, you feel rushed, stressed, or resentful while you cook or eat, even the healthiest dishes can drain your energy. That's why it's important to match your food to the quality of your energy today. Don't take on Mending Moussaka when you're irritable and running short of time: The hot kitchen and warming quality of the dish will only aggravate you and counteract the nourishing qualities of the food. Save that dish for a day

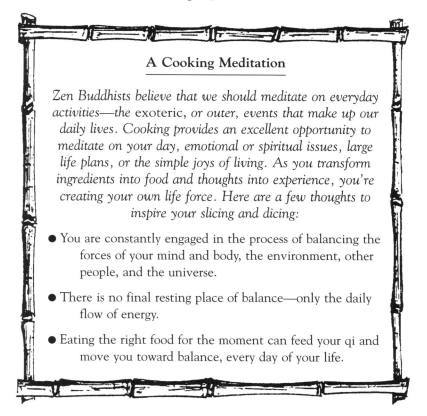

A Cooking Meditation

Zen Buddhists believe that we should meditate on everyday activities—the exoteric, or outer, events that make up our daily lives. Cooking provides an excellent opportunity to meditate on your day, emotional or spiritual issues, large life plans, or the simple joys of living. As you transform ingredients into food and thoughts into experience, you're creating your own life force. Here are a few thoughts to inspire your slicing and dicing:

- You are constantly engaged in the process of balancing the forces of your mind and body, the environment, other people, and the universe.

- There is no final resting place of balance—only the daily flow of energy.

- Eating the right food for the moment can feed your qi and move you toward balance, every day of your life.

when you want to stretch out and warm up the house with a delicious spicy aroma, and seek peace now with something cool and simple, like Crab and Cucumber Salad.

The high regard in which the Chinese hold the *ting*—the sacred ceremonial cauldron in which food is presented at banquets and in the temple of the ancestors—illuminates the pivotal importance of correct cooking and eating in a life well lived. The ting symbolizes taking up the new, and as the wood of the fire is considered to nourish the spirit, the cauldron enables the transformation of food into nourishing renewal by cooking. Because the ting is used to feed both people and gods, it represents the intertwining of the human and the divine through food. The I Ching says:

> Fire over wood:
> The image of the cauldron.
> Thus the superior man consolidates his fate
> By making his position correct.

PART II

THE

FENG SHUI

COOKBOOK

RECIPES

C hoose from the following yin, yang, and balanced recipes to correct your energy, to achieve short-term goals such as gearing up or cooling down, or to activate the mental, physiological, and behavioral powers of the Five Elements. No matter what kind of energy you choose, you'll enjoy all the benefits and pleasures of nourishing yourself with fresh and delicious food.

You might want to refer to the Feng Shui Kitchen Ba Gua on page 8 as a refresher when you read the recipe notes and arrange your feng shui plate. For a list of the recipes according to essential nature, turn to page 217.

Soups

Chicken Soup for a Cold	*balanced*
Gingered Sweet Potato Soup	*yin*
Green Grape Gazpacho	*yin*
Miso Soup	*yin*
Slimming Soup	*balanced*

Salads and Seasonings

Asparagus, Spinach, and Shiitake Salad With Miso Dressing	*yin*
Chili Oil	*yang*
Chinese Chicken Salad	*balanced*
Crab and Cucumber Salad	*yin*
Hot and Sour Mangoes	*balanced*
Lively Lentil Salad	*balanced*
Rice Stick Noodle Salad	*yin*
Ruby Chicken Salad	*yin*
Soft Salad With Orange-Sage Vinaigrette	*yin*
Tomato Timbales With Avocado and Cream	*yin*

Warm Scallop Salad With *balanced*
Green Beans and Almonds
White-Hot Cabbage Slaw *yang*
Yin-Yang Salad *balanced*

Beverages
Fresh Ginger Tea *yang*
Pacific Martinis *yang*
Tamarind Cooler With Lime *yin*
Cubes

Main Courses
Black Bean–Stuffed Chicken *yang*
Breast
Broccoli Bowties *balanced*
Chicken and Daikon in *yang*
Red Wine Sauce
Chili-Honey Barbecued *yang*
Baby Back Ribs
Chilled Tofu With Scallions *yin*
and Sesame Oil
Coconut Shrimp Risotto *balanced*
Crab With Ginger Beurre Brun *balanced*
Drunken Firepot Shrimp *yang*
Eggplant, Tomato, and Chevre *yin*
Tart
Fire-Roasted Filet Mignon *yang*
With Wild Mushroom Sauce
and Arugula Mashed Potatoes
Five-Element Peanut Noodles *balanced*
Flexible Stir-Fry *balanced*

Grapefruit-Poached Sole With *yin*
Watercress Sauce
Grilled Tofu Sandwich *balanced*
Lamb Satay With Peanut Sauce *yang*
Mending Moussaka *yang*
Miso Eggplant *yin*
Mu Shu Chicken Wrap *balanced*
Orange-Braised Tofu *yin*
Oyster Egg Custard *balanced*
Peppered Tuna With Wasabi *yang*
Sauce
Pineapple-Ham-Stuffed Yam *balanced*
Pork and Shrimp Wontons *balanced*
With Cilantro Pesto
Quick Chickpea Curry *yang*
Sake-Glazed Black Cod With *yang*
Ponzu Relish
Salt-Roasted Duckling With *yang*
Beer-Braised Cabbage
Seared Salmon With *yang*
Horseradish Butter
Sensuous Squab *yang*
Sesame Pork Cellophane *balanced*
Noodles
Soba Noodle Platter *yin*
Spicy Sesame Chicken *yang*
Squid Ink Pasta With Calamari *balanced*
and Summer Vegetables
Stuffed Butternut Squash *yin*
Sushi-Style Salmon Tartare *yin*

Tempura du Jour	*yang*	Berry Balsamic Parfaits	*yin*
Thai Tacos	*yang*	Black Brownies	*yang*
		Fire and Ice Sundaes	*balanced*
Desserts		Five-Spice Almond Cake	*yang*
Banana Coconut Cream	*yin*	Green Tea Tofu Flans	*yin*
Pudding		Lime Pie	*yin*

Soups

CHICKEN SOUP FOR A COLD

Balanced

The Stock
   1   roasting chicken, 3½–4 pounds (1½–2 kg)
   4   whole cloves
   3   small onions, peeled
   3   carrots, peeled, trimmed, and quartered
   6   cloves garlic, peeled, trimmed, and lightly smashed with the flat side of a knife
 1″ (2.5 cm) piece fresh ginger, peeled, sliced into coins, and lightly smashed with the flat side of a knife
 10 whole peppercorns
   1   teaspoon salt
 12 cups (3 l) water

The Soup
1–2 tablespoons minced garlic
1–2 tablespoons minced fresh ginger
  2 serrano chili peppers, seeded and minced

4   scallions, sliced
    Salt and freshly ground pepper to taste

1. To make the stock: Rinse the chicken inside and out and place in a large stockpot along with the neck and gizzard.
2. Press the cloves into one of the onions; cut the other onions into quarters. Add the onions, carrots, garlic cloves, ginger slices, peppercorns, salt, and water to the pot. Cover and bring to a boil. Uncover, reduce to a simmer, skim the froth, and cook for 1-1/2 hours, skimming occasionally.
3. Remove the chicken and let cool. Continue to simmer the stock until it's reduced to 2 quarts (2 l), about 1 hour longer. Cool and refrigerate until fat is congealed or overnight.
4. Remove the skin from the chicken and discard. Shred or dice the meat. Cover and refrigerate.
5. To make the soup, skim the fat off the top of the stock. Bring to a boil with the minced garlic and ginger, serrano chilies, and scallions. Add the chicken meat, return to a simmer, and cook for 5 minutes more. Season to taste with salt and pepper. Serve piping hot.

Serves 6 to 8.

The Essence of the Dish

Chinese medicine recommends that you stick to liquids when you have a cold or flu to give your body a break from the challenges of heavy digestion. Liquids also rehydrate mucous membranes to create an unfriendly environment for viruses. And possibly the best liquid you can have when you're sick is old-fashioned chicken soup, which scientifically earns its traditional reputation as a cure-all with the recent identification of cysteines, amino acids that thin mucus to help you breathe easier, as well as a compound that mimics a drug prescribed for respiratory illness, in broth made from chicken. The Chinese also hold that broth nourishes your blood and essence. This soup adds the chicken's meat to the liquid mix, because it's easily digested and boosts immunity in several ways. Protein provides the amino acids that form the building blocks of immune cells, and the meat is rich in iron—which also feeds immune cells—and B vitamins to help those cells divide and enable the synthesis of antibodies.

There's also a full complement of natural cold medicines. Garlic's antibacterial compound, allicin, has made the bulb a favorite in fighting off invaders since ancient times, and ginger is thought to have similar properties as well as aiding digestion in your weakened system. The serrano chilies and scallions both contribute vitamin C, and the chilies act as both a decongestant and an expectorant to help you cough and blow all the bad stuff away. And all four additions burn with intense yang heat to blast the germs out of your body! Not to worry, however: The cooling and moisturizing effect of the broth keeps you from feverishly overheating.

Options and Opportunities

Let's face it: This is a recipe for when you have someone caring for you through your cold. If you're not blessed with a guardian angel willing to wrestle with the stockpot, poach 4 to 6 boneless, skinless chicken breast halves in 8 cups (2 l) of canned chicken broth. Remove the meat and shred or dice, then proceed from step 5.

Adjust the amount of minced garlic and ginger to your taste. The more you add, the stronger your cold medicine, but sick stomachs can be sensitive. Likewise, you can turn the heat up or down by adjusting the quantity of serrano peppers. Asian chili sauce can stand in for fresh peppers if need be—or just add an extra kick for those who really want to sweat it out! If you prefer a brothier soup, reserve some of the cooked chicken for another use.

Complements

When the first symptoms strike, mobilize your army of immune cells with a day of nothing but soup, orange juice, and Fresh Ginger Tea. For best results, sip the soup over a half-hour time period (reheating as necessary) to allow its healing benefits to kick in.

GINGERED SWEET POTATO SOUP   Yin

    1   tablespoon unsalted butter
    2   leeks, white part only, halved vertically, cleaned, and sliced thin
    1   teaspoon minced fresh ginger
    3   cups (750 ml) peeled and diced sweet potatoes (yams) (about 14 ounces,
        400 g, or 1 large)
   3½   cups (875 ml) water
   ½–1 teaspoon salt
    ¾   cup (180 ml) milk
    ½   teaspoon ground ginger
        Dash mace
        White pepper to taste

1. Melt the butter in a soup pot over medium to low heat. Add the leeks and sauté, adding a little water if they start to dry out, until tender but not brown, for about 15 minutes. Add the fresh ginger and cook for another minute or so, until fragrant. Add the sweet potatoes, water, and salt, raise the heat, and bring to a boil. Reduce the heat, partially cover the pot, and simmer until the sweet potatoes yield to your fork, 20 to 30 minutes.

2. Puree the soup in a vegetable mill or food processor. Return to a clean pan and stir in the milk. Season with the ground ginger, mace, white pepper, and additional salt to taste. Reheat just until simmering, then cool, cover, and refrigerate for 4 hours or more.

   Serves 4.

The Essence of the Dish

The Chinese consider all soups moistening and cooling—yin—and Gingered Sweet Potato Soup, made in the style of a vichyssoise and served cold, embodies yin's gentle, accommo-

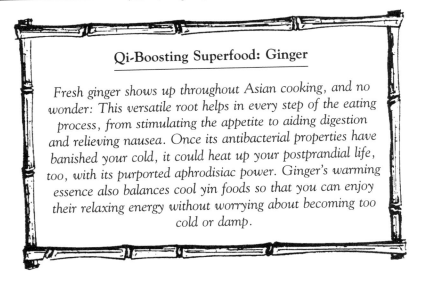

Qi-Boosting Superfood: Ginger

Fresh ginger shows up throughout Asian cooking, and no wonder: This versatile root helps in every step of the eating process, from stimulating the appetite to aiding digestion and relieving nausea. Once its antibacterial properties have banished your cold, it could heat up your postprandial life, too, with its purported aphrodisiac power. Ginger's warming essence also balances cool yin foods so that you can enjoy their relaxing energy without worrying about becoming too cold or damp.

dating flow. The orange color and natural sugars of sweet potatoes belong to Earth, the harmonizing element that represents perfect balance and feeds your generous and meditative side. Chilled and smooth, this soup cools and relaxes your qi.

Meanwhile, your body enjoys the sweet potatoes' superdose of vitamin E, an important antioxidant and immunity booster, and vitamin A, which doubles as an antioxidant and a way to keep your skin healthy and moisturized. And while the soup tastes rich and creamy, each serving contains just 5 grams of fat.

Options and Opportunities

Leeks are gritty, and nothing destroys yin energy faster than sand in the soup. Clean them by trimming off the root ends and green leaves, cutting in half vertically, and rinsing very well under running water, fanning the layers to dislodge dirt.

If you don't have mace on hand, nutmeg will do.

If you like, garnish each bowl with a dollop of sour cream or plain yogurt and a sprinkle of snipped fresh chives.

Complements
Make a cool, elegant luncheon of Gingered Sweet Potato Soup, a baby green salad with walnut oil vinaigrette, and tangy Lime Pie.

The Feng Shui Plate
The soup naturally centers itself in its Earth place in the bowl.

GREEN GRAPE GAZPACHO

Yin-Summer

1   pound (450 g) seedless green grapes
2   cucumbers, peeled, seeded, and cut into pieces
1   green pepper, seeded and cut into pieces
½   onion, cut into chunks
2   tablespoons chopped fresh cilantro
1   tablespoon white wine vinegar
3   tablespoons fresh lime juice
¼   teaspoon ground ginger
¼   teaspoon white pepper
¼   teaspoon salt, or to taste

1. Place the grapes, cucumbers, green pepper, and onion in a food processor and puree. Add the remaining ingredients and process until liquefied (the soup will still be chunky). Adjust the seasonings to taste.
2. Chill for several hours before serving.

Serves 4.

The Essence of the Dish

Summer requires upward- and outward-moving foods to cool your body, detoxify your tissues, circulate blood and qi, and keep you active in the heat. With grapes moving up and green pepper, dried ginger, and white pepper moving out, Green Grape Gazpacho provides the heart energy you need to segue into summer, while Wood from the green color and sour lime juice cleanses and concentrates your qi. The soup is also no-cook, fat-free, and fast, which are always welcome in the slow lazy days of summer.

Options and Opportunities

If you crave a taste of the circulating energy of Metal, add a seeded, coarsely chopped serrano pepper in the first puree.

Complements

For a meal that goes straight from the refrigerator to the table, try this gazpacho as a starter with Eggplant, Tomato, and Chevre Tart or Chilled Tofu With Scallions and Sesame Oil. This is also a balancing beginning to any yang entrée—it tastes something like a margarita salad.

MISO SOUP

2 sheets nori (Japanese seaweed)
1 quart (1 l) water
1 tablespoon instant dashi (Japanese soup stock)
¼ cup (60 ml) yellow miso paste
1 14-ounce (400 g) block soft tofu, patted dry and cut into ½″ (1.25 cm) cubes
2 teaspoons soy sauce
¼ cup (60 ml) thinly sliced scallions

1. Place a dry skillet over medium-high heat and toast each nori sheet until crisp and bright green, 30 seconds to 1 minute per side. With scissors, cut into strips 1-1/2 inches (4 cm) long.
2. In a medium saucepan, bring the water to a boil. Add the dashi and reduce to a simmer.
3. Place the miso paste in a small bowl and gradually stir in about 1/4 cup (60 ml) of the hot dashi until smooth. Add the miso mixture to the pot.
4. Return the soup to a simmer, add the nori, and cook for 1 minute.
5. Add the tofu and soy sauce, return to a simmer, and cook for 2 to 3 minutes more.
6. Ladle the soup into bowls and sprinkle with the sliced scallions.

Serves 4.

The Essence of the Dish

This simple and nourishing soup provides the health benefits of soy and seaweed coupled with soft, warm, comfort-food appeal. The Japanese consider it such a staple that they even drink it for breakfast. The kelp in the dashi is very yin as well as an excellent source of vitamins. Sweet yellow miso adds Earth energy to supplement your qi and heal your spleen; the productive elemental cycle continues with Metal (the white tofu) and Water (the salty soy and dashi).

Options and Opportunities

Be aware that many dashi mixes contain MSG (a natural derivative of kelp, which is part of the stock base). If you're sensitive to MSG or can't find dashi, you can leave it out and substitute vegetable, chicken, or beef broth for the water. Likewise, the nori can be omitted if it's hard to find. In either case you'll miss the recipe's traditional taste of the sea, but can still enjoy the sweet tang of miso in this healthful and versatile preparation.

This version is thick with tofu; if you like it with more broth, leave some of the tofu out.

Complements

This soup makes a nice starter to serve with any other yin recipe, or you can serve it as an appetizer to a yang dish for a balanced meal. Or enjoy it alone as a light and low-fat meal!

SLIMMING SOUP

Balanced

½ cup (125 ml) pearl barley
1 cup (250 ml) water
1 onion, chopped
3 cloves garlic, minced
1 tablespoon (15 ml) minced fresh ginger
1 carrot, peeled and diced
1 parsnip, peeled and diced
1 rutabaga, peeled and diced
1 leek, white part only, halved vertically, rinsed well, and chopped
2 cups (500 ml) finely shredded cabbage
7 cups (1.7 l) chicken or vegetable broth
¼ teaspoon ground nutmeg
⅛ teaspoon cayenne pepper or more to taste
¼–½ teaspoon salt
  Freshly ground pepper

1. Soak the barley in the water for 6 hours or up to overnight.
2. Combine the onion, garlic, ginger, carrot, parsnip, rutabaga, leek, and cabbage in a large saucepan. Add the chicken broth, bring to a boil, and reduce to a simmer. Partially cover and cook for 1/2 hour.
3. Add the barley and soaking water and continue to cook until tender, about 20 to 25 minutes more.
4. Stir in the nutmeg, cayenne pepper, and salt and pepper to taste.

   Serves 4 to 5.

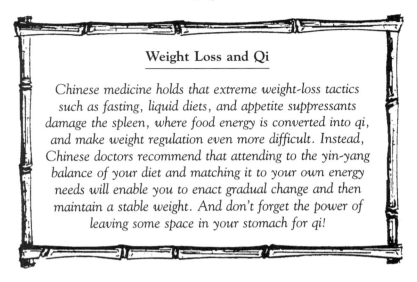

Weight Loss and Qi

Chinese medicine holds that extreme weight-loss tactics such as fasting, liquid diets, and appetite suppressants damage the spleen, where food energy is converted into qi, and make weight regulation even more difficult. Instead, Chinese doctors recommend that attending to the yin-yang balance of your diet and matching it to your own energy needs will enable you to enact gradual change and then maintain a stable weight. And don't forget the power of leaving some space in your stomach for qi!

The Essence of the Dish

Chinese nutritional doctors recommend eating soup when you're trying to trim off pounds, and this hearty potage, jam packed with richly flavored root vegetables, has everything you need to get you on the slimming track. The complex carbohydrates in the vegetables and barley provide satisfaction and energy, while their fiber fills you up. The cabbage adds more tummy-filling bulk along with important vitamins to keep you feeling good. The barley not only strengthens the spleen and prevents cancer but is a mild diuretic to help you detoxify as well. The soup's liquid flushes away the toxins created by burning fat and keeps your stomach full. And the cayenne pepper? It provides a hit of spicy heat that can boost your metabolism for up to three hours after your meal! At just 166 calories and 1 gram of fat per generous 2-cup (500 ml) serving, Slimming Soup satisfies as much as it spurs a dip into your fat stores.

Options and Opportunities

For an even more delicious soup, use the homemade broth from Chicken Soup for a Cold instead of canned broth. Add an extra dash of cayenne pepper to amp up that metabolic burn!

Complements

For the first week of your regime, start every day with a light breakfast, such as cereal with milk and fruit. Lunch is a big, steaming bowl of Slimming Soup. For dinner, opt for grilled fish or skinless chicken breast and vegetables (see also low-calorie recipes such as Sushi-Style Salmon Tartare, Grilled Tofu, and Sake-Glazed Black Cod With Ponzu Relish). Drink plenty of water and tea.

Salads and Seasonings

ASPARAGUS, SPINACH, AND SHIITAKE SALAD
WITH MISO DRESSING

Yin

1   pound (450 g) asparagus, rinsed, with tough ends snapped off
1   tablespoon peanut oil
3   ounces (85 g) shiitake mushrooms, rinsed, stemmed, and sliced ¼″ (.5 cm) thick
1   scallion, minced
6   ounces (170 g) fresh spinach, stemmed, well washed, and dried

The Miso Dressing
4   teaspoons Dijon mustard
2   egg yolks
2   tablespoons yellow miso paste
1   tablespoon soy sauce
1   tablespoon fresh lemon juice
1   tablespoon rice vinegar
1   tablespoon peanut oil
    Salt and white pepper to taste

1. Bring a large pot of salted water to a boil. Add the asparagus and cook until just tender, about 6 to 8 minutes. Drain and refresh with cold water. Chill until ready to serve.
2. Make the Miso Dressing: In a small bowl or glass measuring cup, whisk together the mustard and egg yolks. Whisk in each of the remaining ingredients in order. Season to taste with salt and pepper. Cover and chill until ready to serve.
3. At serving time, heat 1 tablespoon peanut oil in a small nonstick skillet over medium-high heat. Add the shiitakes and minced scallion and sauté, stirring, until tender, a few minutes. Season to taste with salt and pepper.
4. Toss the spinach with 2 tablespoons of the dressing and arrange a bed on each plate. Top with the asparagus spears and drizzle the remaining dressing over them. Sprinkle with the mushrooms and serve.

Serves 4 to 6 as a first course or 2 to 3 as an entrée.

The Essence of the Dish

The prevalent element of this salad is Wood. The green of the vegetables, the tang of the dressing, and the delicacy of the asparagus all reflect Wood's image of springtime, daybreak, and growth. This vital Wood energy enhances the dynamics of family and health in your life, while in your behavior it helps guide your growth by enabling you to listen to others, reflect, and formulate your own opinions.

When it comes to health, Popeye had it right: Spinach is simply one of the best vegetables you can eat, and this salad offers a good dose of calcium and folate (both crucial for pregnant and nursing moms!), and vitamins A and C. Chinese medicine finds that asparagus helps eliminate heat in the body to move you toward a cool yin state.

Options and Opportunities

The contrast between hot and cold when you serve the asparagus chilled and the mushrooms right out of the pan is delightful. On the other hand, when sautéed in advance and chilled before serving, the mushrooms acquire an even more velvety texture. Either way you win.

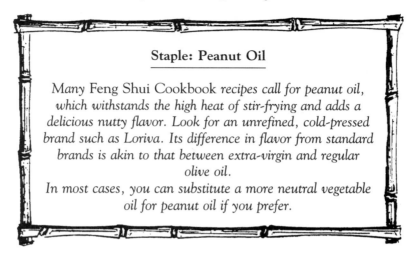

Staple: Peanut Oil

Many *Feng Shui Cookbook* recipes call for peanut oil,
which withstands the high heat of stir-frying and adds a
delicious nutty flavor. Look for an unrefined, cold-pressed
brand such as Loriva. Its difference in flavor from standard
brands is akin to that between extra-virgin and regular
olive oil.
In most cases, you can substitute a more neutral vegetable
oil for peanut oil if you prefer.

Prewashed salad bags of fresh spinach are a great convenience; one will yield the 6 ounces (170 g) you need for this recipe.

Raw eggs pose a risk of salmonella. You can make the egg yolks in the Miso Dressing safer by cooking them in the microwave on high for 30 seconds, then continuing to cook for 10-second intervals until you see the yolks start to move (within 60 seconds total). Cook for 10 seconds more, then remove and beat until smooth with a clean (important!) fork. Return to the microwave and cook until you see movement again (about 5 to 10 seconds). Let them stand for 1 minute and proceed with the recipe.

Complements

You can serve the salad as a first course with Chilled Tofu With Scallions and Sesame Oil for a light yin meal with good nutritional balance and a three-element productive series: Metal, Water, and Wood. Or make it an opener to Eggplant, Tomato, and Chevre Tart for the productive but cool synergy of Wood and Fire.

The Feng Shui Plate

Garnish the top of the plate with something red—crunchy radishes, cooked beets, or roasted red peppers—to provide Fire, the next element after Wood in the productive cycle. If you're serving the salad as a side dish, place it on the left side of the plate in Wood's gua.

CHILI OIL   Yang

   1 cup (250 ml) dried red chili peppers
   1 cup (250 ml) peanut oil

1. Coarsely chop the peppers in a small food processor or spice grinder.
2. Combine the peppers and oil in a nonreactive saucepan and place over medium-low heat. Simmer at 225° F (107° C; use a deep-frying or candy thermometer) for 15 minutes. Remove from the heat and cool.
3. Strain the oil and pour it into a clean glass bottle. Store out of the light at room temperature.

     Yields 1 cup (250 ml).

The Essence of the Dish
Add intense yang and Metal energy to any dish with this high-voltage oil. In pasta or stir-fries, on pizzas, in soups and salads, or drizzled on meats or fish, Chili Oil heats up whatever you eat—fast! Metal can also help you face depression (as can the endorphins that scientists think hot chilies might stimulate) and relieve stagnation. Break out your Chili Oil whenever you're feeling slow, blank, or too careful.

Options and Opportunities
Vary the oil—and further boost its yang rating—with any of the following additions: the zest of an orange, a few peeled garlic cloves, some coins of fresh peeled ginger, or 2 tablespoons

CHINESE CHICKEN SALAD

Balanced

1   pound (500 g) boneless, skinless chicken breasts

The Dressing
1   teaspoon minced fresh ginger
2   cloves garlic, crushed
2   scallions, minced
¼   cup (60 ml) soy sauce
2   tablespoons rice vinegar
2   tablespoons balsamic vinegar
2   tablespoons light brown sugar
¼   teaspoon salt
¼   teaspoon white pepper
1   tablespoon peanut oil
1   tablespoon sesame oil
¼–½ teaspoon chili oil (see recipe on page 73, or purchase in the Asian section of the supermarket)

The Salad
2   stalks celery, sliced
6   cups shredded napa cabbage (about 12 ounces, or 340 g)
1   8-ounce (225 g) can sliced water chestnuts, drained and rinsed
¼   cup (125 ml) bean sprouts
2   tablespoons toasted sesame seeds

1. Fill with water a skillet large enough to hold the chicken breasts in a single layer, and bring to a low boil. Add the chicken, adjust the heat to a low simmer, and poach until cooked through, about 4 minutes per side. Set aside to cool in the liquid.

2. For the dressing, mix together the ginger, garlic, scallions, soy sauce, vinegars, brown sugar, salt, and pepper. Whisk in the oils. Set aside to blend the flavors.
3. Bring a small pot of salted water to a boil and blanch the celery for 30 seconds. Drain and rinse with cold water.
4. Slice the chicken. In a large bowl, combine the chicken with the celery, cabbage, water chestnuts, bean sprouts, and dressing. Toss well. Let stand for 5 to 10 minutes and serve sprinkled with the sesame seeds.

Serves 4.

The Essence of the Dish

The perfect balance of tender chicken breast with light, crunchy vegetables and sweet-and-sour dressing has made Chinese Chicken Salad an American classic. It's also classically good for you: rich in cell-building protein from the chicken and phytochemicals from the cabbage, while also, in this version, low in fat. Yang meat and yin vegetables meet in the middle for a fresh and tasty union.

All of the Five Flavors are here, too—sweet brown sugar, sour vinegar, bitter cabbage, spicy chili oil, and salty soy sauce. With the Five Elements talking directly to your taste buds, you are truly eating in balance.

Options and Opportunities

You can vary the ingredients of the salad for convenience or a change of pace. Think crunch: jicama, thinly sliced carrots (blanch with the celery), peeled and seeded cucumber, julienned peppers. But if you substitute iceberg lettuce for the cabbage you'll lose a lot of life-extending nutrients! Resist the urge to skip blanching the celery, which brings out its flavor and bright green color and creates a friendlier texture.

Complements

Iced tea is nice with this salad. Finish your meal with some almond cookies—light, and bearers of good luck.

The Feng Shui Plate

Serve this Earth-toned creation in the center of a large, brightly colored plate for contrast.

CRAB AND CUCUMBER SALAD

Yin

2 tablespoons mayonnaise
1 teaspoon rice vinegar
   White pepper to taste
1 6-ounce (170 g) can crabmeat, drained (or fresh crabmeat, picked over)
½ cucumber, peeled and sliced thin
½ teaspoon salt
2 teaspoons toasted sesame seeds (or *norigoma furikake,* Japanese seaweed and sesame seed seasoning)

1. Combine the mayonnaise, vinegar, and white pepper. Stir 2/3 of the dressing into the drained crabmeat and chill.
2. Meanwhile, arrange the cucumber slices in a colander and sprinkle with the salt. Let stand for 5 minutes. Rinse under running water, drain, and pat dry on paper towels.
3. Toss the cucumbers with the remaining 1/3 of the dressing and arrange in concentric circles on two plates. Mound the crab mixture on top, sprinkle with the sesame seeds or *furikake,* and serve.

Serves 2.

The Essence of the Dish

Crab, cucumber, and sesame seeds are all quintessentially yin, so this cool salad is a must for hot weather or when you feel hot under the collar. Its pure white color evokes Metal, which combines with the calming effect of yin to prepare you to make well-reasoned critiques without being harsh or unfair. Crab's salty essence contributes Water's ability to sharpen your intuition, soften your words, and connect with other people, so try this recipe when diplomacy is needed.

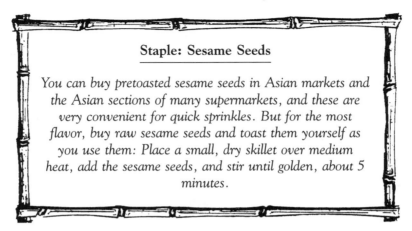

Staple: Sesame Seeds

You can buy pretoasted sesame seeds in Asian markets and the Asian sections of many supermarkets, and these are very convenient for quick sprinkles. But for the most flavor, buy raw sesame seeds and toast them yourself as you use them: Place a small, dry skillet over medium heat, add the sesame seeds, and stir until golden, about 5 minutes.

Options and Opportunities

Slice the cucumbers thin so that they become very pliant after salting. The salt imparts an appealing soft texture to the cucumbers, but don't neglect to rinse it off or you might go into sodium shock. For an ultra-yin vegetarian dish, replace the crabmeat with the rest of the cucumber and serve the salad on a bed of lettuce—another cooling food.

Complements

Complete your cooldown with a tart lime sorbet to add Wood to your productive string.

HOT AND SOUR MANGOES **Balanced**

2 mangoes, peeled and pitted
3 limes
  Chili oil (see recipe on page 73, or purchase in the Asian section of the supermarket)

1. Cut one of the limes into 4 wedges and reserve for garnish. Arrange the mangoes on 4 plates and squeeze lime juice generously over the top to taste. Drizzle with chili oil (be careful, it's hot!). Add a lime wedge to each plate and serve.

   Serves 4.

The Essence of the Dish
This surprising combination of sweet, sour, and hot will wake up your taste buds to a whole new level of consciousness. Tart and juicy, it can moisten your qi if you're too yang and dry (irritable), while the chili oil can warm you up if you're too yin and cool (chilled or feeling wishy-washy). Meanwhile, the superfruit mango antes up its antioxidants—vitamins A and C—to extend your life, feed your eyes, and boost your immune system.

Options and Opportunities
Adjust the lime juice and chili oil to taste. Bring the chili oil to the table; you might find yourself drizzling on more and more. . . .

Complements
Serve Hot and Sour Mangoes as a salad course, an accompaniment to grilled meats or seafood, or a light dessert with a kick.

The Feng Shui Plate
The sweet orange mango belongs in Earth's spot on the center of the plate.

LIVELY LENTIL SALAD

Balanced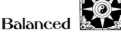

1½   cups (375 ml) dried lentils, rinsed
1   carrot, peeled and diced
1   red onion, diced
2   cloves garlic, minced, divided
¾   teaspoon salt, divided
1   bay leaf
4   teaspoons red wine vinegar
    Dash cayenne pepper
4   tablespoons extra-virgin olive oil
1   cucumber, peeled, halved, and thinly sliced
5   radishes, thinly sliced
    Arugula leaves
    Freshly ground black pepper to taste

1. Combine the lentils, carrot, onion, 1 clove garlic, 1/2 teaspoon of the salt, and bay leaf in a large pot. Cover with water and bring to a boil. Reduce to a simmer and cook, partially covered, until tender, 25 to 30 minutes.
2. While the lentils are cooking, combine the vinegar, remaining minced garlic clove, remaining 1/4 teaspoon salt, and cayenne pepper. Whisk in the olive oil. Pour over the cucumber and radishes, toss, and marinate for 15 to 20 minutes. Arrange a small bed of arugula leaves on each plate.
3. When the lentils are done, drain and remove the bay leaf. Add the cucumber and radishes with their marinade and fresh black pepper. Adjust the salt to taste. Toss well to combine. Serve on the arugula warm, at room temperature, or chilled.

Serves 4 as a main course or 8 as a side dish.

The Essence of the Dish

This hearty salad features the energy of Fire, manifested in the pleasantly bitter flavor of cucumber, radishes, and arugula, as well as red in the vegetables and vinegar. Fire stimulates circulation and is good for the cardiovascular system—as are the lentils, whose soluble fiber sweeps arteries clean of plaque deposits, and olive oil, which raises beneficial HDL cholesterol levels and lowers those of bad LDL cholesterol, which can build up on arterial walls and bring your circulation to a standstill. Fire is the element of fame, joy, and the sun, and Lively Lentil Salad keeps your heart beating at its peak as you pursue your wildest dreams.

Options and Opportunities

The salad's flavors develop as it sits, but it's also nice warm from the pot.

Complements

For a vegetarian feast with complete protein, serve the salad with Stuffed Butternut Squash. You can also complement the lentils' protein with a loaf of whole-grain bread. The salad makes a nice meal with a soup to start, or it can accompany any grilled meat or fish.

The Feng Shui Plate

Arrange the lentils from the center out toward the top part of the plate with the arugula tucked under the left-hand border and extending out into Wood's gua. With the brown lentils and orange carrots activating Earth's energy, you have a productive series of Wood, Fire, and Earth. As a side dish, position the salad at the top of the plate.

RICE STICK NOODLE SALAD   Yin

The Nuoc Cham Dressing
¼   cup sugar
½   cup (125 ml) hot water
¼   cup (60 ml) fish sauce
2   tablespoons fresh lime juice
1   clove garlic, minced
1   jalapeño pepper, seeded and minced

The Salad
6   ounces (170 g) dried rice stick noodles
2   carrots, peeled and finely grated
1½   cups (375 ml) bean sprouts
1   cup (250 ml) packed mint leaves, coarsely chopped
½   cup (125 ml) packed cilantro leaves, coarsely chopped
4   leaves Boston or butter lettuce

1. To make the Nuoc Cham Dressing, dissolve the sugar in the hot water. Stir in the fish sauce, lime juice, garlic, and jalapeño. Let stand at room temperature to blend flavors.
2. Bring a large pot of salted water to a boil and cook the noodles until they rise to the top and are just tender, 2 to 5 minutes. Drain and rinse thoroughly with cold water.
3. In a large bowl, toss together the noodles, carrots, bean sprouts, mint, and cilantro. If necessary, use your hands to evenly disperse the ingredients. Add the Nuoc Cham Dressing and toss again. Cover and chill until you're ready to serve.
4. To serve, place a lettuce leaf cup on each plate and fill with the noodles.

Serves 4.

The Essence of the Dish

Absolutely fat-free, this unusual Vietnamese-inspired salad spotlights pure and pungent flavors. The green herbs and sour lime juice contribute a concentrated dose of Wood energy, good for cleansing your qi, toning your nerves, and tuning up your liver. Cilantro is considered a cure for an upset stomach, so this detoxifying dish might be just the trick when you've overindulged. And that spunky fish sauce?—a good source of B vitamins and protein.

Options and Opportunities

Choose the best leaves from your head of lettuce to serve as cups for the noodles. Boston or butter lettuce gives you an edge over iceberg with its extra vitamin C and beta carotene.

Complements

Add some protein to your meal with a first course of Miso Soup, or create a balanced meal by serving the salad as a first course to a yang meat or seafood entrée.

The Feng Shui Plate

Bolster the energy of Wood by garnishing the left side of the plate with sprigs of fresh herbs and a wedge of lime.

Ruby Chicken Salad
Yin

1   pound (450 g) boneless, skinless chicken breast halves
½   cup (125 ml) diced celery
1   cup (250 ml) seedless red grapes, halved
½   red grapefruit, peeled, sectioned, membranes removed, and pulled into bite-size pieces
¼   cup (60 ml) chopped, toasted pecans
½   cup (125 ml) crème fraîche
¾   teaspoon salt
¼   teaspoon black pepper
1   teaspoon minced lemon zest

1. Poach the chicken in simmering water until cooked through, about 4 to 5 minutes per side. Remove, cool, and cut into 1/2″ (1.25 cm) chunks.
2. Combine the chicken, celery, grapes, grapefruit, and pecans in a bowl. Add the crème fraîche, salt, pepper, and lemon zest and combine thoroughly. Chill for several hours. Adjust the seasonings to taste and serve.

Serves 4.

The Essence of the Dish
Cool your heart fires with this soft, lightly sweet, and creamy dish. The gentle simmering of the chicken imparts yin energy; raw celery cools, consolidates, and relaxes your qi; the grapes and grapefruit create a perfect sweet-and-sour complement. The colors and flavors of Wood (green celery, sour grapefruit), Fire (red fruit), Earth (sweet grapes), and Metal (white crème fraîche) form a productive series for any time you want to keep your cool and balance.

Options and Opportunities

Crème fraîche is a thick cultured cream, less sour than sour cream and simply delicious. If you can't find it in the dairy section of your supermarket, you can make it at home: Heat 1 cup (250 ml) heavy cream to 100° F (37° C, just above lukewarm), stir in a tablespoon (15 ml) buttermilk, transfer to a clean glass or plastic container, and let sit at room temperature for 12 to 36 hours until thickened and slightly tart. Refrigerate until ready to use. You can use sour cream instead as a shortcut, and consider using a reduced-fat version if you want to lighten this dish.

Complements

Counter the richness of Ruby Chicken Salad with delicate Green Tea Tofu Flans for dessert.

The Feng Shui Plate

With the balance of elemental colors and flavors and the richness of this salad, it's best to serve it mounded on small plates—perhaps glass or crystal to set off the jewel tones.

SOFT SALAD
WITH ORANGE-SAGE VINAIGRETTE

Yin

The Orange-Sage Vinaigrette
1 shallot, chopped
1 tablespoon Dijon mustard
1 tablespoon chopped fresh sage
1 orange, zested and juiced
4 tablespoons rice vinegar
4 tablespoons extra-virgin olive oil
Salt and pepper to taste

The Salad
1 ripe mango, peeled, pitted, and diced
1 small cantaloupe, peeled, seeded, and diced or cut in balls
1 ripe pear, peeled and diced
1 ripe avocado, peeled and diced
4 plum tomatoes, seeded and diced

1. To make the Orange-Sage Vinaigrette, whisk together the chopped shallot, Dijon mustard, sage, 1 teaspoon orange zest, 4 tablespoons (60 ml) orange juice, and vinegar. Gradually whisk in the olive oil. Season to taste with salt and pepper and set aside.
2. In a large bowl, gently combine the mango, cantaloupe, pear, avocado, and tomatoes. Add the vinaigrette and toss carefully.

Serves 4.

The Essence of the Dish

Soft Salad is a lesson in fragility and the precarious balance among sweet, savory, and sour that could be said to summarize life. As you eat, imagine yourself like these pliant fruits: water within, fresh and flowing with the productive current of Wood (avocado, vinegar), Fire (tomato, sage, mustard), and Earth (mango, cantaloupe, orange juice). As sweet innocence is tempered with the bitter wisdom of sage, so Soft Salad traces the mythic journey from spring and dawn (Wood), through maximum productivity (Fire), and to the point of perfect balance (Earth).

Meanwhile, 1 cup (250 ml) of cantaloupe gives you all the vitamin A, in the form of the antioxidant beta carotene, that you need in a day, and mangoes lavish you with vitamins A and C. The tomatoes weigh in with their own antioxidant, lycopene, and add the anti-carcinogens p-coumaric acid and chlorogenic acid. The potassium in cantaloupe, avocado, and tomatoes keeps your blood pressure in check, while in the Chinese medicine chest, orange peel is thought to cure fevers and coughs and clear up your skin. It is a good journey!

Options and Opportunities

Use only the softest, ripest fruits, substituting others in season if necessary.

Complements

Soft Salad is the perfect first or following course to yang dishes such as Black Bean–Stuffed Chicken Breast, Peppered Tuna With Wasabi Sauce, or Sensuous Squab. Or enjoy a relaxing yin meal with Grapefruit-Poached Sole With Watercress Sauce.

The Feng Shui Plate

For a Five-Element presentation, cover the top, left, and center of the plate with the salad. Crumble a little white goat or feta cheese in Metal's right gua, and strew a few black olives or peppercorns in Water's spot at the bottom.

TOMATO TIMBALES WITH AVOCADO AND CREAM — Yin

1¾ (430 ml) cup tomato juice, divided
  1 envelope plain gelatin
  ½ teaspoon sugar
  1 bay leaf
  4 teaspoons fresh lemon juice, divided
  ¼ teaspoon salt
  ¼ teaspoon black pepper
  1 ripe avocado, skinned and pitted
  ¼ cup (60 ml) sour cream

1. Combine 3/4 cup (180 ml) of the tomato juice, the gelatin, sugar, and bay leaf in a medium saucepan. Place over medium heat and stir until the gelatin dissolves.
2. Remove from the heat, remove the bay leaf, and stir in the remaining tomato juice, 2 teaspoons of the lemon juice, and the salt and pepper. Pour into 4 custard cups and chill until firm.
3. At serving time, blend the avocado, remaining 2 teaspoons lemon juice, and salt and pepper to taste in a food processor. Spoon a circle of avocado puree onto each of 4 plates.
4. Loosen the timbales by dipping the cups into hot water and running a knife around the edges. Unmold onto the puree and top each with a spoonful of sour cream. Serve at once.

Serves 4.

The Essence of the Dish

This cool, yielding combination has a hidden strength in the gelatin—a reminder that to yield is not to melt and that softness can maintain its own shape. Tomatoes and avocados are both female fruits, underscoring the dish's yin energy to take you within. And the complementary colors of Wood and Fire burn a cool but vital flame.

Options and Opportunities

You can prepare the timbales well in advance of serving; just be sure to wait until the last minute to puree the avocado so that it doesn't become discolored.

Complements

This is the perfect first course to transition you from the outer-directed activity of the day to the quieter and more intimate space of evening. Follow with whatever serves your energy needs.

The Feng Shui Plate

The green, red, and white color scheme is beautiful to behold and, when you serve it in Earth's gua in the center of the plate, creates a productive sequence of Wood, Fire, Earth, and Metal.

WARM SCALLOP SALAD
WITH GREEN BEANS AND ALMONDS

Balanced

¼ cup (60 ml) red wine vinegar
¼ cup (60 ml) soy sauce
1 teaspoon minced fresh ginger
1 shallot, minced
5 tablespoons olive oil, divided
Freshly ground black pepper to taste
1 pound (450 g) green beans, cut into 2" (5 cm) pieces on the diagonal
Pinch salt
¼ cup (60 ml) sliced almonds
1 pound (450 g) bay scallops
4 cups (1 l) baby greens

1. For the dressing, combine the vinegar, soy sauce, ginger, and shallot. Whisk in 4 tablespoons (60 ml) of the olive oil and season with fresh black pepper. Set aside to blend flavors.
2. Bring a large pot of water to a boil and add the green beans and a pinch of salt. Cook until bright green and just tender, about 8 minutes. Drain and refresh thoroughly with cold water, tossing the beans with your hands under the stream of water to stop the cooking process.
3. Place a skillet over medium-high heat, add the almonds, and toss for a few minutes until toasted. Remove and set aside. Add the remaining tablespoon of olive oil to the skillet. When it's hot, add the scallops and sauté, stirring, until they're firm and just cooked through, about 2 minutes. Add the green beans and toss to heat through. Remove from the heat and season with salt and pepper.
4. To serve, toss the greens with 1/2 the dressing and arrange on plates. Toss the scallop mix-

ture with the remaining dressing, serve onto the greens, and sprinkle with the almonds.

Serves 4.

The Essence of the Dish
This balance of warm and cool, land and sea, salty and sour offers delicate flavors and textures to help you find the beauty in nuance. You'll also benefit from the good qi of a full creative cycle: Metal (white scallops and almonds, ginger), Water (dark, salty soy sauce), Wood (green vegetables and sour vinegar), Fire (the red of the vinegar), and Earth (the sweetness of the scallops and their finished earthy color). Suitable for a dinner party or a quick weeknight meal, this dish celebrates the good, easy, and elegant things in life.

Options and Opportunities
You can cook the beans and make the dressing in advance and refrigerate. Bring both back to room temperature before proceeding.

Supermarket scallops are all too often plumped up with a lot of water. If yours exude a lot of liquid in the sauté, drain them before adding the beans to the pan.

Complements
Try starting your meal with a yin cooldown of Gingered Sweet Potato Soup and finishing with Black Brownies cut into triangles and dusted with confectioners' sugar.

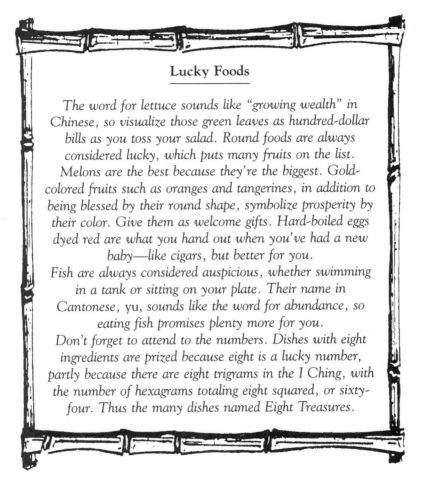

Lucky Foods

*The word for lettuce sounds like "growing wealth" in
Chinese, so visualize those green leaves as hundred-dollar
bills as you toss your salad. Round foods are always
considered lucky, which puts many fruits on the list.
Melons are the best because they're the biggest. Gold-
colored fruits such as oranges and tangerines, in addition to
being blessed by their round shape, symbolize prosperity by
their color. Give them as welcome gifts. Hard-boiled eggs
dyed red are what you hand out when you've had a new
baby—like cigars, but better for you.*

*Fish are always considered auspicious, whether swimming
in a tank or sitting on your plate. Their name in
Cantonese, yu, sounds like the word for abundance, so
eating fish promises plenty more for you.*

*Don't forget to attend to the numbers. Dishes with eight
ingredients are prized because eight is a lucky number,
partly because there are eight trigrams in the I Ching, with
the number of hexagrams totaling eight squared, or sixty-
four. Thus the many dishes named Eight Treasures.*

WHITE-HOT CABBAGE SLAW

Yang

1   small green cabbage (1½–2 pounds, 675–900 g), quartered, cored, and thinly sliced crosswise
1   white onion, halved lengthwise and thinly sliced into half rings
2   tablespoons white wine vinegar
1   tablespoon soy sauce
2   tablespoons sugar
2   teaspoons minced fresh ginger
1   teaspoon Chinese chili sauce, or to taste
½   cup (125 ml) coarsely chopped walnuts
4   slices bacon
3   tablespoons peanut oil
1   tablespoon roasted sesame oil
⅓   cup (80 ml) white wine
   Salt and freshly ground pepper to taste

1. Combine the cabbage, onion, vinegar, soy sauce, sugar, ginger, and chili sauce in a large bowl and toss well. Set aside to marinate for a few minutes.
2. Place your largest skillet over medium heat. Add the walnuts and toast, tossing occasionally, until fragrant, about 5 minutes. Remove from the pan and set aside.
3. Place the bacon in the pan and return it to medium heat. Fry, turning frequently, until crisp. Remove to paper towels. Drain the bacon fat from the pan but don't wipe it clean.
4. Add the peanut and sesame oils to the pan and increase the heat to medium high. Add the cabbage mixture and toss until coated and sizzling.
5. Add the wine, reduce the heat to medium, cover the pan, and cook, stirring occasionally, until the cabbage is tender, about 8 minutes more. Uncover the pan and, if necessary, raise the heat to cook off excess liquid.

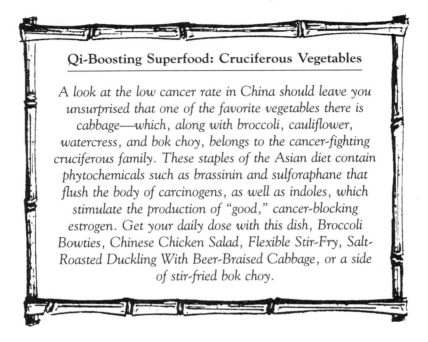

Qi-Boosting Superfood: Cruciferous Vegetables

A look at the low cancer rate in China should leave you unsurprised that one of the favorite vegetables there is cabbage—which, along with broccoli, cauliflower, watercress, and bok choy, belongs to the cancer-fighting cruciferous family. These staples of the Asian diet contain phytochemicals such as brassinin and sulforaphane that flush the body of carcinogens, as well as indoles, which stimulate the production of "good," cancer-blocking estrogen. Get your daily dose with this dish, Broccoli Bowties, Chinese Chicken Salad, Flexible Stir-Fry, Salt-Roasted Duckling With Beer-Braised Cabbage, or a side of stir-fried bok choy.

6. Remove from the heat and crumble in the bacon. Add the walnuts and toss. Season to taste with salt and freshly ground pepper, toss again, and serve.

Serves 4 as a main course or 8 as a side dish.

The Essence of the Dish

White-Hot Cabbage Slaw is unpretentious food filled with the white-and-spicy, stimulating energy of Metal. Yang heat comes from the chili sauce, ginger, wine, and walnuts (which are considered good for the brain, perhaps because of their physical resemblance to it). Ginger warms the blood; the nuts provide cholesterol-lowering omega-3 oils; and the cabbage, onions, and ginger contribute life-extending phytochemicals. Meanwhile, Metal's circulatory power makes good qi flow and strengthens your psychic backbone. Try White-Hot Cabbage Slaw when you need to take a stand.

Options and Opportunities

You can make this dish vegetarian by omitting the bacon; you may want to add a bit more oil and an extra handful of walnuts. You can save time with the packaged, preshredded cabbage available in the supermarket. If it won't all fit into the pan at once, stir in a little at a time—it shrinks as it softens. If you don't have Chinese chili sauce, substitute crushed red pepper.

The Feng Shui Plate

The simple white tones of this dish are set off best by serving it on a big colored plate. Alternatively, serve half portions as a side dish with grilled meat, fish, or poultry. Place the slaw at the right side of the plate, in Metal's west gua.

YIN-YANG SALAD

Balanced

2   tablespoons fresh lemon juice
1   large shallot, minced
2   cloves garlic, crushed
2   teaspoons ground coriander
1   teaspoon salt
2   tablespoons olive oil
    Freshly ground black pepper to taste
1   14-ounce (400 g) block regular tofu, well pressed and cut into ½″ (1.25 cm) cubes
1   15-ounce (425 g) can black beans, drained and rinsed
½   cup (125 ml) diced water chestnuts

1. To make the dressing, combine the lemon juice, shallot, garlic, coriander, and salt. Whisk in the olive oil and season with black pepper to taste.
2. In a large bowl, combine the tofu, beans, and water chestnuts. Pour the dressing over and toss gently to combine. Chill until ready to serve.

    Serves 5 to 6 as a side dish or first course, or 3 to 4 as a main dish.

The Essence of the Dish

This portrait in black and white embodies the balance of yin and yang both by its colors and by its textural contrast of firm black beans to soft, yielding tofu. It's also a powerful yin-yang health tonic for both genders. For women, the phytoestrogens in the tofu and black beans help prevent breast and uterine cancer and may protect against female trouble such as the loss of bone mass and the symptoms of menopause. Men, who are at greater risk for heart disease than women until their later years, will particularly appreciate the cholesterol-lowering effect of tofu, black beans, olive oil, and garlic. This simple dish is a quick step toward countering the hazards of your sex and attaining the balance of good health.

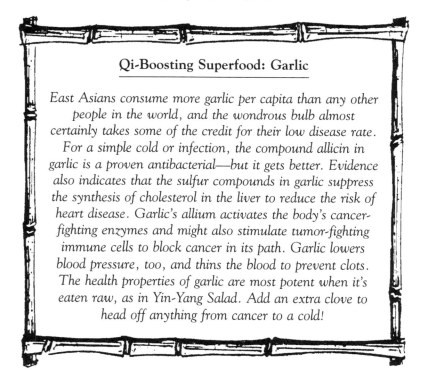

Qi-Boosting Superfood: Garlic

East Asians consume more garlic per capita than any other people in the world, and the wondrous bulb almost certainly takes some of the credit for their low disease rate. For a simple cold or infection, the compound allicin in garlic is a proven antibacterial—but it gets better. Evidence also indicates that the sulfur compounds in garlic suppress the synthesis of cholesterol in the liver to reduce the risk of heart disease. Garlic's allium activates the body's cancer-fighting enzymes and might also stimulate tumor-fighting immune cells to block cancer in its path. Garlic lowers blood pressure, too, and thins the blood to prevent clots. The health properties of garlic are most potent when it's eaten raw, as in Yin-Yang Salad. Add an extra clove to head off anything from cancer to a cold!

Worried about the raw garlic? Water chestnuts are thought to sweeten the breath!

Options and Opportunities

The texture of regular tofu is nicer than that of firm for this raw presentation, but it's important to press the water out to help the cubes maintain their shape when you toss the salad (see page 115). The flavors develop as the salad sits, so this is a good make-ahead recipe.

If you'd like to expand the color scheme to all Five Elements, omit the water chestnuts and add seeded chopped tomato, yellow pepper, and fresh cilantro. Now the focus is more on elemental balance than yin and yang.

Complements
While this salad makes a satisfying meal by itself (try it as a take-along lunch), you can also serve it as an accompaniment to grilled white seafood (halibut, scallops, and the like) to continue the color scheme and maintain balanced qi.

The Feng Shui Plate
This intermingling of yin and yang is auspicious on any part of the plate.

Beverages

FRESH GINGER TEA

Yang

6 cups (1.5 l) water
3" (7.5 cm) piece fresh ginger, peeled and sliced into coins

1. Bring the water to a boil. Add the ginger coins, reduce the heat to low, and cook for 10 minutes more.
2. Strain out the ginger and serve.

Serves 4.

The Essence of the Dish

This is not your grandmother's gentle herbal tea out of a bag! Fresh Ginger Tea is a spicy, stimulating tonic for your mind and body that offers a quick hit of yang heat anytime you need to warm up. And by giving your digestive system an assist, the tea helps you metabolize food into energy to put you at your peak.

Options and Opportunities
For a stronger kick, add a few more slices of ginger and let the tea steep a bit longer. If you'd like, sweeten your tea with a little honey for a serotonin-induced mood boost.

Complements
Drink this alongside any yang dish as an additional hit of heat, or sip it with yin foods to prevent them from making you chilled. Follow any meal with a cup of Fresh Ginger Tea to circulate the energy of food through your body and help you reap its natural energy harvest.

Ginseng: A Lively Boost to a Long Life

Another caffeine-free tea favored for its stimulating powers is ginseng, made from a root the Chinese particularly admire for its humanlike shape. Ginseng is considered to strengthen the qi of the entire body and promote longevity—and can be so stimulating that Chinese doctors won't prescribe the stronger American-grown variety for anyone with high blood pressure. (If you suffer from hypertension, you might want to check the origins of any ginseng you ingest.) You can buy ginseng tea in many supermarkets, Asian markets, health food stores, and tea shops.

PACIFIC MARTINIS

Yang

1	orange, washed
1	star anise
1	stick cinnamon
1	whole clove
¼	teaspoon fennel seeds
2	coins peeled fresh ginger
1	dried red chili pepper, split vertically, or pinch red pepper flakes
1	750-milliliter bottle of vodka

1. Using a zester or a sharp knife and working in a spiral, peel a long strip of zest from the orange. Be careful to take only the orange-colored zest, not the white skin underneath.
2. Add the orange zest, spices, ginger, and red chili pepper to the bottle of vodka and let it steep at room temperature overnight.
3. Freeze the bottle for at least 8 hours before serving. Serve in chilled martini glasses.

Serves 12.

The Essence of the Dish
Neutral vodka serves as a showcase for the flavors of Chinese Five Spices, plus a kick of chili. Though icy cold and amber clear, this drink is fired with intense yang energy from the alcohol and spices. Sip judiciously.

Options and Opportunities
If you like, you can mix the drinks like classic martinis with dry vermouth to taste. For a striking party presentation, freeze the bottle of vodka in a cardboard ice cream carton filled with water. Loosen the carton from the ice with hot water, peel the carton away, and serve

the vodka in its ice (be sure to leave the bottle neck exposed so you can pick it up and pour).

   If you plan to store the vodka for more than twenty-four hours after freezing, you may want to decant it into another bottle to remove the spices and prevent it from getting too strong.

TAMARIND COOLER WITH LIME CUBES   Yin

3   ounces (100 g) tamarind pods or prepared, block-form tamarind pulp (about ⅓ cup,
    or 80 ml, pulp)
4   cups (1 l) water, divided
⅓   cup (80 ml) sugar

The Lime Cubes
2   limes
1½ cups (375 ml) water

1. To prepare fresh tamarind pods, pull off the strings and remove the skins.
2. Bring 3 cups (750 ml) of the water to a boil and add the peeled tamarind pods or pulp
   and the sugar. Stir, reduce to a simmer, and cook for 5 minutes. Remove from the
   heat and steep at room temperature for 2 hours.
3. To make the Lime Cubes, use a paring knife to cut the peel from one of the limes and
   slice it into thin strips. Squeeze the juice from both limes, strain, and mix with the
   water. Drop 2 strips of peel into each compartment of a 16-cube ice cube tray, pour in
   the juice mixture, and freeze.
4. Strain the tamarind mixture into a pitcher, pressing hard on the solids to allow the pulp
   to pass through. Add the remaining 1 cup (250 ml) water and chill until you're ready
   to serve. Serve over the Lime Cubes.

   Serves 4.

The Essence of the Dish
Infused with the sour yin energy of Wood, tamarind is thought to cool fevers, quench thirst,
and heal the liver and kidneys. Wood energy gathers and cleanses your qi and assists in the

decision-making process. Try this hydrating cooler anytime you're feeling warm, dry, dissipated, or wishy-washy.

Options and Opportunities

Tamarind pods and blocks of prepared tamarind pulp can be found in Asian, Latin, and Middle Eastern markets. The blocks of pulp save you a step, but purists claim the best tamarind flavor comes directly from the pods. If you have more than 2 hours to allow for the infusion, cover the mixture and refrigerate for up to 24 hours before straining.

Adjust the sugar to your own taste; the sourer the drink, the more Wood it is.

Use Lime Cubes to add a cool dash of Wood energy to any drink!

Complements

This is a quick cooler on its own, or a refreshing accompaniment to any meal. Serve it with other yin recipes to enhance their effects, or use it as a balancing libation for yang dishes. Made on the sour side, Tamarind Cooler can complement a meal the way a glass of wine can—without the hot yang energy or side effects of alcohol.

Main Courses

BLACK BEAN-STUFFED CHICKEN BREAST

Yang

- 4 bone-in chicken breast halves with skin and rib meat
- ¼ cup (60 ml) Chinese black bean garlic sauce
- 1 teaspoon soy sauce
  Black pepper
- 1 scallion, minced
- ½ cup (125 ml) dry sherry
- ½ cup (125 ml) chicken broth
- 2 tablespoons (¼ stick) unsalted butter, cut into bits

1. With your fingers, loosen the skin from the top of each chicken breast half, leaving it as whole and attached as you can. Spread each half underneath the skin with 1 tablespoon (15 ml) of the black bean garlic sauce. Place the chicken skin-side up in a roasting pan, rub with the soy sauce, and season with black pepper. Set aside to marinate while you preheat the oven to 500° F (260° C).
2. When the oven is hot, roast the chicken for 10 minutes, then reduce the heat to 350° F (177° C) and baste the chicken with the pan juices. Roast for 15 to 20 minutes more, basting once or twice, until cooked through and the juices run clear.

3. Remove the chicken from the pan and tent with foil to keep it warm. Place the roasting pan over medium-high heat on the stove (use 2 burners if it's large) and stir in the minced scallion. Sauté for a moment, then add the sherry and broth, stirring up any brown bits. Boil, stirring constantly, until reduced to a syrup, a few minutes. Reduce the heat to low and whisk in the butter, one piece at a time.
4. Serve the chicken with the sauce.

Serves 4.

The Essence of the Dish

This dish is the black and salty essence of Water. By dissolving congealed qi and supplementing your blood and essence, the Water in Black Bean–Stuffed Chicken combines with yang energy to make you motivated, powerful, and attractive for important business or social contacts.

Options and Opportunities

If you'd like to balance the potentially argumentative force of Water now, add one each red, green, and yellow peppers, seeded and sliced thin, to the roasting pan alongside the chicken (remove them with the chicken before making the sauce). Combined with the chicken's white meat, you now have a full feng shui palette.

This dish is also delicious cold. Rewarm the sauce in the microwave at 50 percent power or over low heat on the stove for dipping or drizzling.

Complements

Viognier, a complex white wine with layers of fruit and flowers, can stand up to the strong flavors of the dish and add some yang power of its own.

The Feng Shui Plate

Place the chicken in Water's gua at the bottom of the plate. If you've added roasted peppers to the dish, scatter them over the remaining guas.

BROCCOLI BOWTIES

Balanced

3   heads (about 2 pounds, or 900 g, total) broccoli, cut into small florets, stems discarded or reserved for another use (about 6 cups, or 1.5 l, florets)

8   ounces (225 g) dried bowtie pasta (farfalle)

2   tablespoons peanut oil

4   scallions, sliced

4   cloves garlic, minced

1   teaspoon minced fresh ginger

   Pinch red pepper flakes

4   tablespoons oyster sauce

1   tablespoon roasted sesame oil

2   tablespoons (¼ stick) unsalted butter

¼   teaspoon salt

   Freshly ground black pepper to taste

1. Bring a large pot of water (with a pasta basket, if you have one) to a boil. Salt generously, return to a boil, and add the broccoli. Blanch until just tender, about 4 to 5 minutes. Remove with the pasta basket or a slotted spoon.
2. Add the pasta to the boiling water and cook according to package directions.
3. Meanwhile, heat the peanut oil in a wok or large skillet over high heat. Add the scallions, garlic, ginger, and red pepper flakes and stir. Add the broccoli and stir-fry until cooked through, a few minutes. Remove from the heat and add the oyster sauce, sesame oil, butter, salt, and pepper to taste. Stir until the butter is melted.
4. Drain the pasta, reserving about 1 cup (250 ml) of the cooking water. Add the pasta to the broccoli and toss well to combine, adding some cooking water to moisten if necessary. Serve.

Serves 4.

The Essence of the Dish

This quick and simple vegetarian dish boasts classic flavor combinations and the good health that a balanced life brings. Broccoli is a good source of calcium—which not only strengthens bones but also appears to lower blood pressure—iron, and the antioxidant vitamins A and C. The cruciferous family that broccoli belongs to also contains cancer-fighting phytochemicals.

Dominated by Water (wheat, salty oyster sauce) and Wood (green)—neighbors in the creative cycle that both act to concentrate qi—Broccoli Bowties unite Wood's cleansing power with Water's ability to soothe and soften to make this a good detox dish, a way to gather in diffuse energies and put them all in one place for the next adventure.

Options and Opportunities

Throw in an extra head of broccoli if you're a big fan. You can't hurt yourself with this superfood! Save your broccoli stems to make a cream of broccoli soup or a broccoli puree later in the week.

The butter in this recipe serves to round out the flavors and coat the pasta, but if saturated fat is a great concern for you at the moment, you can replace all or part of it with peanut or sesame oil—or nothing, according to your tastes and needs.

Complements

To up your protein count and continue the oyster theme, start with Oyster Egg Custard in appetizer portions.

The Feng Shui Plate

Arrange the pasta over the bottom and left side of the plate in the areas of Water and Wood. Complement Fire and Metal with an arc of sliced tomatoes sprinkled with Chili Oil (page 73) from the top to the right side of the plate.

CHICKEN AND DAIKON IN RED WINE SAUCE   Yang

1	pound (450 g) boneless, skinless chicken thighs, cut into ¾" (2 cm) chunks
	Salt and pepper
2	tablespoons (¼ stick) unsalted butter, divided
8	ounces (225 g) daikon, peeled, trimmed, and cut into ¾" (2 cm) chunks
1	medium onion, cut into ¾" (2 cm) chunks
1½	cups (375 ml) chicken broth
½	cup (125 ml) red wine
1½	tablespoons soy sauce
1½	tablespoons sugar
1	tablespoon mirin (sweet Japanese cooking wine)

1. Season the chicken well with salt and pepper. Melt 1 tablespoon of the butter in a large saucepan over medium-high heat and add the chicken. Brown lightly on all sides and remove from the pan.
2. Add the daikon and onion to the pan and toss for a minute or two until well coated. Add the chicken broth, cover, and bring to a boil. Uncover, reduce the heat to medium high, and continue boiling, stirring occasionally, for 10 minutes more. Add the red wine, soy sauce, sugar, and mirin and continue to cook for another 10 minutes.
3. Return the chicken to the pan, reduce the heat to medium, and simmer for about 5 minutes more, until the chicken is cooked through and the liquid is reduced. Remove from the heat and swirl in the remaining tablespoon of butter. Adjust the salt and pepper to taste. Serve into bowls.

Serves 4.

The Essence of the Dish

This easy and elegant stew features Fire—in the process of boiling and reduction over the flame, the pleasantly bitter flavor of the daikon (a radishlike root vegetable), and the red color

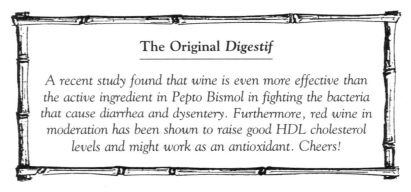

The Original *Digestif*

A recent study found that wine is even more effective than the active ingredient in Pepto Bismol in fighting the bacteria that cause diarrhea and dysentery. Furthermore, red wine in moderation has been shown to raise good HDL cholesterol levels and might work as an antioxidant. Cheers!

of the wine. It can dry and strengthen you on a cold, damp day, and provide the mix of assertion and wisdom you need to get things done. For a dish of such deep, rich flavor, it's a wise nutritional choice, too, with a relatively low fat count. The daikon helps you digest the modest amount of butter in the recipe; add the root to any rich dish for this assimilative boost.

Don't try this when you're feeling quick tempered or critical! The Fiery radish might unleash your tongue.

Options and Opportunities
Daikon is a long, white root vegetable available in most supermarkets. Its flavor mellows significantly as it cooks, but be sure to try any leftovers grated raw as a peppy garnish. If you don't have mirin, you can substitute sake or sherry and add an extra pinch of sugar.

Complements
Lively Lentil Salad and a glass of the wine you use in the stew further fuel the Fire, or you can go for greater balance with a green salad and some crusty bread. If you prefer to use your yang energy to get on quickly to other things, enjoy this on its own as a one-pot, one-dish meal.

The Feng Shui Plate
Stew has no choice but to sit in the middle of the bowl—which is perfect for the Earth tones of this finished dish.

Chili-Honey Barbecued Baby Back Ribs — Yang

4 scallions
1 tablespoon minced garlic
1 tablespoon minced fresh ginger
¼ cup (60 ml) honey
1 tablespoon Chinese chili sauce
½ cup (125 ml) soy sauce
½ cup (125 ml) sake
1 tablespoon roasted sesame oil
½ teaspoon ground cinnamon
3 pounds (1.3 kg) baby back pork ribs
½ cup (125 ml) water

1. Trim the green stems of the scallions and reserve. Mince the white bulbs and mix with the garlic, ginger, honey, chili sauce, soy sauce, sake, sesame oil, and cinnamon.
2. Arrange the ribs in a single layer in a nonreactive pan or bowl. Pour the marinade over, cover, and let marinate for 1 hour at room temperature or, preferably, in the refrigerator overnight, turning a few times.
3. Preheat the oven to 350° F (177° C). Place the ribs and marinade in a baking dish, cover with foil, and roast until the meat is starting to pull away from the ends of the bones, 45 minutes. Turn the ribs a few times as they roast.
4. Meanwhile, trim the tops off the reserved onion stems. Make a vertical cut from the top of each stem to about 1 1/2 inches (3.75 cm) from the bottom. Place in a bowl of ice water and refrigerate.
5. Preheat the grill or broiler. Remove the ribs from the baking dish. Place the dish with the cooking juices over medium heat (use 2 burners if it's large) until the liquid starts to bubble, then deglaze with the water. Cook, stirring up the brown and caramelized bits, until reduced to a syrup, a few minutes.

6. Grill or broil the ribs until brown, 4 to 5 minutes on the first side, 3 to 4 minutes on the second. Serve topped with the sauce and garnished with the crisp scallions.

Serves 4.

The Essence of the Dish

Rich, dark, sweet, hot, and salty, this dish imparts a broad spectrum of yang energy and a productive flavor series of Earth, Metal, and Water. Gnawing on the bones with juice running down your chin returns you to your primeval self. Try it when you're preparing for a daring feat or daunting challenge.

Complements

Brush assorted vegetables with some peanut oil and grill them while the ribs bake.

When you crave yang energy but also want to be able to slow down to go to sleep, try starting with Chili-Honey Barbecued Baby Back Ribs, then following with a refreshing salad course of Hot and Sour Mangoes, whose balanced energy transitions you toward the softer side. Finish with Green Tea Tofu Flans, a cool, creamy yin dessert that will send you sweetly into dreamland.

The Feng Shui Plate

Place the dark and salty ribs in Water's gua at the bottom of the plate, with the green onion garnish above, in the left-hand area of Wood. If you've also grilled vegetables, arrange them over the rest of the plate according to their elemental colors.

CHILLED TOFU WITH SCALLIONS AND SESAME OIL Yin

½ block regular or soft tofu (7 ounces, or 200 g)
1   scallion, sliced thin
1   tablespoon soy sauce
1   teaspoon roasted sesame oil

1. Pat the tofu dry and place on a small plate. Sprinkle the scallion over the tofu. Drizzle first with the soy sauce, then with the sesame oil.
2. If desired, chill until ready to serve.

   Serves 1.

The Essence of the Dish

This superfood preparation is powered by two adjacent elements in the productive cycle: Metal (the white tofu), which enhances the flow of qi and promotes recovery, and Water (the dark, salty soy sauce), which concentrates qi and elicits maximum repose. It's also the essence of simplicity—fast food with a difference to cool you down during or after a hectic, too-yang day. And with the greater bean at the center, it spares you fat and calories while heaping on healthful phytoestrogens. With this simple dish, you could prevent breast, ovarian, and endometrial cancers; lower your cholesterol; slow calcium loss from bones; and alleviate the symptoms of menopause. Not bad for fast food!

Options and Opportunities

Experiment with the proportions of scallion, soy sauce, and sesame oil to find your favorite mix. The dish is best after the tofu has had a little time to absorb the other flavors, so put it together, pop the plate in the refrigerator, and take a half an hour or so to enjoy your favorite soft music, a relaxing bath, or a phone call to a friend. You'll sit down with the yin energy already flowing.

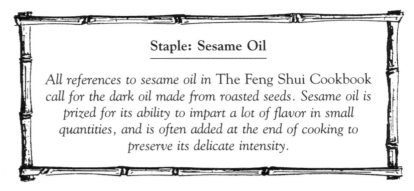

Staple: Sesame Oil

All references to sesame oil in The Feng Shui Cookbook *call for the dark oil made from roasted seeds. Sesame oil is prized for its ability to impart a lot of flavor in small quantities, and is often added at the end of cooking to preserve its delicate intensity.*

Complements

Thinly slice some cucumber and toss with a splash of rice vinegar and a pinch of sugar. Let marinate briefly in the refrigerator.

This also makes a delightful appetizer served with sesame or rice crackers with a knife for slicing.

QI-BOOSTING SUPERFOOD: SOY

The Chinese word for soybean translates as "greater bean"—and a soy-rich diet is surely one of the primary reasons Asians boast such clean bills of health. With phytoestrogens to block breast cancer; genistein to kill cancer cells of all sorts; a host of other life-extending phytochemicals such as isoflavones, saponins, protease inhibitors, and phenols; mainstream nutrients including complete vegetable protein, iron, phosphorus, potassium, and calcium; and the power to lower bad LDL cholesterol levels and boost good HDL, ease the symptoms of menopause, and increase bone density—what food could be more super than soy?

And what superfood could be less appreciated by Western cooks and eaters?

The easiest and most rewarding way to eat soy may be in the form of the much-maligned tofu. If you're tofu averse, read on to discover that a little bean curd savvy goes a long way. Your qi will thank you for the leap of faith you take to try it out.

Freshness

Like any simple food, the quality of tofu is of paramount importance (think of the difference between spongy commercial bread and a loaf of freshly baked artisanal sourdough), so shop around for a brand you like and eat it while it's fresh. Buy tofu with a freshness date stamped on the package, and in the case of vacuum-sealed packages, don't wait for an expiration day that may be months in the future! Once you've opened the package, store the tofu submerged in water that you change every day, and eat it within a week.

Pressing

Tofu is 80 to 85 percent water, which beats even the human body, and the resulting soft texture is an initial problem for some cooking procedures. Fortunately, this is easily solved by pressing. Wrap your tofu in paper towels or clean dish towels, place in a rimmed plate or pan, place another plate or pan on top, and weight with a few cans, a skillet, or any handy heavy object. Let this sit for 20 minutes to an hour, depending on how much time you have, and drain off the accumulated water every so often. The smaller the piece, the longer you press, the heavier your weight, and the more frequent your draining, the firmer your tofu will be. You can even change towels a few times if you're a fanatic. In general, any pressing, even 5 minutes' worth, helps tofu retain its shape and absorb other flavors, so do what works for

your schedule and palate. Some dishes benefit from tofu's naturally soft texture—for instance, Miso Soup—and don't require pressing.

Firmness
Buy firm tofu for grilling or broiling, soft for soups, soft or regular for raw dishes such as Chilled Tofu With Scallions and Sesame Oil or Yin-Yang Salad, and regular for other uses. Beware of extra-firm and some brands of firm tofu, which are so coagulated they become rubbery and lack the velvety texture and subtle flavor that are tofu's special assets. It's worth taking the time to press the water out of the soft or regular type for a more delicate result. Not all tofu brands are alike, and Japanese-style brands are, as a rule, softer than Chinese-style.

Freezing
Freezing tofu actually improves its texture by helping it shed excess water, though the process transforms its pure white color to a meatier tan. Press the tofu, marinate it if you like, wrap it well, and freeze at least overnight and preferably for a few days. You can quick-thaw frozen tofu by placing it in a pan, covering it with boiling water, and letting it stand for about 10 to 15 minutes. Rinse it in cold water and pat it dry. You can freeze tofu in slices and use it as is, or crumble a defrosted block and use it like ground meat. The chewy results are particularly appealing to avowed carnivores.

Another point in tofu's favor: It's easy to digest. And not to worry. Even the Chinese disagree upon whether tofu itself has any flavor—but this makes it all the more valued for its ability to absorb and blend the flavors of the foods it's cooked with. Think of it as the food of Zen.

COCONUT SHRIMP RISOTTO

Balanced

2 cups (500 ml) chicken broth
½ pound (225 g) small raw shrimp in the shell
1 tablespoon peanut oil
1 small onion, chopped
1 cup (250 ml) canned coconut milk (not cream of coconut)
1 cup (250 ml) Arborio rice
½ cup (125 ml) dry white wine
¼ cup (60 ml) frozen corn kernels, thawed
¼ cup (60 ml) frozen peas, thawed
¼ cup (60 ml) coarsely chopped cashews
Dash cayenne
Salt and freshly ground pepper

1. Bring the chicken broth to a low boil in a skillet wide enough to hold the shrimp in a single layer. Add the shrimp and poach until just firm and pink, stirring to turn, about 3 to 5 minutes. Remove the shrimp with a slotted spoon, reserving the liquid, and let cool. Strain the broth through cheesecloth into a small saucepan. Peel the shrimp and set aside.
2. Heat the peanut oil in a heavy saucepan over medium heat. Add the onion and cook until softened and translucent, 5 minutes. Meanwhile, add the coconut milk to the reserved broth and place over low heat.
3. Add the rice to the onions and sauté until it looks pearly, about 1 minute. Add the white wine and cook until the liquid is almost evaporated. Add 1/2 cup (125 ml) of the hot broth-and-coconut-milk mixture and simmer, stirring frequently and adjusting the heat as necessary, until the liquid is almost all absorbed. Continue to add the broth mixture 1/2 cup (125 ml) at a time, stirring and simmering until the liquid is almost absorbed, the rice is just tender, and the broth is almost used up.

4. With the last addition of liquid, add the shrimp, corn, and peas. Cook until creamy; the rice should be soft but still intact.
5. Remove from the heat and stir in the cashews, cayenne, a generous amount of salt, and pepper to taste. Serve at once.

Serves 4, unless you are very hungry.

The Essence of the Dish

The making of risotto demonstrates synergy between the opposing elements of Water and Fire. When in proper relation, these elements produce steam energy to cook the rice to perfection—as in the Chinese character depicting qi. But there is tension and danger in the arrangement. If the Fire flames too hot, the Water evaporates and the dish burns; if the Water boils over, the Fire is extinguished. Making risotto requires that you constantly moderate the heat and the addition of liquid, maintaining optimal conditions and watching carefully to prevent misfortune. It's a good life lesson.

A harmonious blend of shrimp and wine (yang in nature), broth (yin), and rice (neutral), Coconut Shrimp Risotto embodies equilibrium. Internalize this energy balance as you create the visual image of qi in your kitchen.

Options and Opportunities

You can save time by using cooked shrimp and skipping step 1, resulting in a slightly less flavorful broth. By all means use fresh corn and peas if you have them! Add them a little earlier in the cooking process. If you'd prefer a vegetarian dish, substitute vegetable for chicken broth, omit the shrimp, and increase the vegetables and cashews.

To dress up the dish, add a garnish of 1/2 cup (125 ml) flaked sweetened coconut tossed with a good dash of cayenne pepper and toasted in a 350° F (177° C) oven for about 5 minutes. Sprinkle over each plate of risotto.

Complements

Try a subtle Sauvignon Blanc, such as the Bernardus Monterey County. Add a crunchy salad and perhaps a sliver of zesty Lime Pie to finish.

The Feng Shui Plate

Serve the risotto on a black plate and you'll have a full feng shui palette—green peas, pink shrimp, white coconut rice, and yellow corn, all on a dramatic black background. You'll rebalance just looking at it.

CRAB WITH GINGER BEURRE BRUN

Balanced

 2 cups (500 ml) dry white wine
 ¼ cup (60 ml) balsamic vinegar
 1 tablespoon minced fresh ginger
 1 tablespoon minced shallot
 ½ cup (1 stick) unsalted butter, cut into pieces
   Salt and pepper to taste
 2 whole Dungeness crabs, cooked, cracked, and chilled

1. Combine the wine, vinegar, ginger, and shallot in a small saucepan. Bring to a boil, reduce the heat to medium, and simmer until reduced to a glaze.
2. Remove from the heat and gradually whisk in the butter. Season with salt and pepper to taste. Serve at once as a dipping sauce for the crab.

Serves 4.

The Essence of the Dish

In China, crab is an exalted delicacy, considered very romantic—and when eaten with warming ginger and wine, this very cool food becomes a symbol of ultimate balance. While this is traditionally accomplished by dipping the crab into a ginger-vinegar sauce and drinking wine alongside, this Ginger Beurre Brun puts the wine right into the sauce and complements the sweet flavor of the crab with rich and elegant style.

   This is a celebratory dish for a special occasion, representing all Five Elements with its flavors or colors and evoking harmony between heaven and earth.

Options and Opportunities

The Chinese prefer a she-crab, especially one that's plump with roe. Ask your fish purveyor to crack the crab; you'll still need a cracker to finish the job at the table. Serve the sauce in an individual ramekin for each person, and prepare for a hands-on dining experience.

If you'd prefer a more traditional dipping sauce without any added fat, mix 1/4 cup (60 ml) each soy sauce and balsamic vinegar with 1 tablespoon minced fresh ginger. Let this steep for a while before serving.

Complements
Tomato Timbales With Avocado and Cream make a perfect salad, served either as a first course or alongside. For a feast, balance the yin of the timbales with thin slivers of Five-Spice Almond Cake for dessert. This is an auspicious meal indeed.

The Feng Shui Plate
Place a ramekin of sauce in the center of each plate, where its brown color activates Earth, and arrange the crab legs around it in spokes. Place the crab bodies on a plate (gold plates are preferred for serving crab in China) in the center of the table and let people break off pieces as they wish for the prized snowy flesh inside.

DRUNKEN FIREPOT SHRIMP

Yang

          2   tablespoons (¼ stick) unsalted butter
          2   tablespoons olive oil
          1   red onion, halved lengthwise and sliced thin vertically
          6   large cloves garlic, minced
       1½   cups (375 ml) fish stock or clam juice
        ¾   cup (180 ml) dry white wine
     ½–1   teaspoon red pepper flakes
        ½   teaspoon salt
       1½   pounds (675 g) large shrimp (31–35 per pound, or per 450 g), peeled, and deveined
                if you wish
          2   Roma tomatoes, seeded and chopped
        ¼   cup (60 ml) chopped Italian parsley
                Freshly ground black pepper

1. Heat the butter and oil in a stockpot over medium heat. Add the onion and sauté until softened and slightly caramelized, about 10 minutes. Add the garlic and stir until fragrant, 1 to 2 minutes more.
2. Stir in fish stock or clam juice, wine, red pepper flakes, and salt, raise the heat, and bring to a boil.
3. Add the shrimp, tomatoes, and parsley and simmer over medium heat, stirring occasionally, until the shrimp are just cooked through, 5 minutes. Grind in some fresh black pepper and adjust the salt and red pepper to taste. Serve into bowls.

Serves 4.

The Essence of the Dish

This is not strictly a firepot, in which each guest cooks individual portions of meat and vegetables at the table in a central pot of broth, like fondue—but the stew is Fiery and it's made in a pot! Shrimp is a food warm in essence, and here it teams with wine and red pepper for an intense yang experience.

Metal and Fire, spicy and red, ensure that this dish will make you lively, stimulated, and circulating faster than the speed limit. Drunken Firepot Shrimp is food to elicit assertive opinions; try it for a loud dinner party.

Options and Opportunities

You can devein the shrimp if you like: After you've removed the shell, pull or cut out the thin blue vein running down the back. But this time-consuming task yields only a small benefit in aesthetics that will be lost in the stew of the pot, and Fire energy doesn't nurture patience for such details.

Complements

You need some crusty sourdough bread to sop up the juices, and perhaps some roasted red peppers tossed in vinaigrette to serve as a cool salad.

The Feng Shui Plate

Place the bowl on a large dinner plate with the roasted red pepper salad at the top for one more burst of Fire, and a hunk of bread to the right in Metal's quadrant.

Eggplant, Tomato, and Chevre Tart   Yin

½ pound Roma tomatoes (225 g, about 3), thinly sliced
1 shallot, chopped
1 pound Japanese eggplant (450 g, or 4–5), sliced on the diagonal into ¼″ (.5 cm)
   rounds
   Olive oil
2 eggs
¾ cup (180 ml) milk
½ teaspoon salt
   Dash nutmeg
   Freshly ground pepper
1 deep-dish 9″ (23 cm) pie shell
1 5-ounce (140 g) package soft goat cheese
1 cup packed fresh spinach leaves (about 1½ ounces, or 50 g), chopped fine

1. Arrange the tomatoes on a plate in a single layer and sprinkle with the chopped shallot
   and salt and pepper to taste. Set aside to marinate.
2. Position the broiler rack about 3 inches (7.5 cm) from the heat and preheat the broiler.
   Generously brush 2 baking sheets with olive oil and arrange the eggplant slices in a
   single layer. Brush the eggplant with additional oil to coat and season with salt and
   pepper.
3. Broil the eggplant until the tops are lightly browned, about 3 minutes. Flip, season the
   other sides, and broil until browned, about 2 minutes more. Remove from the broiler
   and set the oven to 375° F (190° C).
4. In a small bowl, lightly beat the eggs. Whisk in the milk, salt, nutmeg, and freshly ground
   pepper to taste.

5. Layer 1/2 the eggplant in the pie shell and crumble 1/2 the goat cheese over it. Top with 1/2 the tomatoes, leaving behind any liquid accumulated on the plate, then sprinkle with all the spinach. Repeat the eggplant, goat cheese, and tomato layers, then carefully pour in the custard.
6. Bake the tart for 45 to 50 minutes, until the custard is set and the crust is golden brown. Cool the tart completely on a rack, then chill until ready to serve.

Serves 4.

The Essence of the Dish

Eggplants and tomatoes are particularly yin members of the plant world because they're seed-bearing females. Their biological function is borne out in their appearance. Compare their soft, rounded shapes, for instance, to a long, hard carrot. Spinach is also a very cool vegetable and adds some high-potency vitamins and minerals. The colors of the tart form a creative series for your eyes: white custard (Metal), black eggplant (Water), green spinach (Wood), and red tomatoes (Fire).

This tart can bring out your feminine side when you want to contemplate, reflect, or open yourself up to new ideas. Cut a wedge and chill out.

Options and Opportunities

If you're using a frozen piecrust in a thin aluminum pan, protect against spills by placing a baking sheet underneath. You can adjust the amount of olive oil to your taste and dietary goals; a generous hand will yield the softest, most tender eggplant.

Complements

Toss a few additional fresh spinach leaves with lemon juice or vinegar (whose sourness reinforces the green color for extra Wood energy) and a bit of olive oil.

The Feng Shui Plate

Place the tart wedge, colored red by the tomato, at the top of the plate (the ba gua's southern home of Fire) with the point to the center, and garnish with the spinach salad on Wood's left-hand side.

FIRE-ROASTED FILET MIGNON WITH WILD MUSHROOM SAUCE AND ARUGULA MASHED POTATOES

Yang

The Arugula Mashed Potatoes

1½ pounds (675 g) Idaho potatoes, peeled and quartered
2 packages (⅔ ounce, or 18 g, each) arugula
¾ cup (180 ml) hot milk, or more as needed
2 tablespoons (¼ stick) softened unsalted butter
   Salt and pepper to taste

The Steaks

4 filet mignon steaks, about 1 pound (450 g) total
1 teaspoon balsamic vinegar
1 teaspoon soy sauce
1 teaspoon olive oil
   Salt and pepper
2 tablespoons (¼ stick) unsalted butter
1 large shallot, chopped
6 ounces (170 g) fresh shiitake mushrooms, stemmed and sliced ¼" (.5 cm) thick
1½ cups (375 ml) red wine
1 cup (250 ml) chicken broth
½ cup (125 ml) heavy cream

For the potatoes

1. Place the potatoes in a large saucepan and add water to cover. Salt lightly, bring to a boil, cover loosely, and boil until the potatoes are very tender, about 10 to 15 minutes.
2. Meanwhile, bring a smaller pot of water to a boil and blanch the arugula leaves until dark green, about 45 seconds. Drain thoroughly in a colander, then transfer to a food processor and puree.

3. When the potatoes are done, drain them and return them to the pot. Shake them over medium heat for about 15 seconds to dry them out, for better texture. Remove from the heat.

4. Add about 2 tablespoons of the hot milk to the pan and beat with an electric mixer at medium speed until smooth. Continue to add the hot milk, alternating with the butter, in 2 rounds. Beat in the arugula puree. Season generously with salt and freshly ground pepper. Keep warm.

For the steaks

1. Put the steaks on a plate and rub all over with the balsamic vinegar and soy sauce, then the olive oil. Season both sides with salt and pepper and set aside to marinate at room temperature. Prepare the grill or preheat the broiler.

2. Melt the butter in a medium sauté pan over medium-high heat. Add the shallot and mushrooms and a sprinkle of salt and give a good stir. Sauté, stirring occasionally, until the mushrooms have emitted and reabsorbed their liquid.

3. Deglaze the pan with the red wine, scraping up brown bits from the bottom and boiling for several minutes until the liquid is reduced by 1/2—it will be syrupy and the mushrooms will look quite drunk. Reduce the heat to medium.

4. Add the stock and cream and simmer the sauce gently until it is reduced by 1/2, about 10 minutes. Season to taste with salt and pepper.

5. Meanwhile, grill or broil the steaks for about 2 minutes per side for rare (the yang way). If you prefer, continue to cook the steaks to desired doneness at the edge of the grill, or reduce the oven thermostat to 375° F (190° C) and move them to the middle rack. Serve with the sauce.

Serves 4.

The Essence of the Dish

The red color of the beef and wine and the arugula's subtle bitter edge conjure up Fire—fame, energy, joy, and the heart. This is a dish of power, celebration, and bright sun. It's rich in protein to build cells in your body and release alertness chemicals such as norepinephrine in your brain for alertness and creativity. Bright acidic notes in the wine reduction

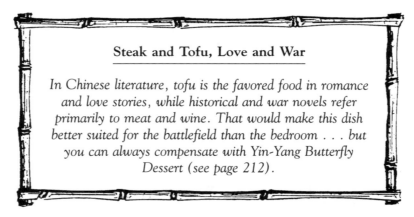

Steak and Tofu, Love and War

In Chinese literature, tofu is the favored food in romance and love stories, while historical and war novels refer primarily to meat and wine. That would make this dish better suited for the battlefield than the bedroom . . . but you can always compensate with Yin-Yang Butterfly Dessert (see page 212).

and balsamic vinegar underscore the richness of the filet mignon and cream; wild mushrooms taste undomesticated and free; and the roasted meat is a primeval symbol of yang masculinity.

Fire-Roasted Filet Mignon is the stimulating food of the doer. Create and eat it with confidence and energy.

Options and Opportunities

The dish is rich because yang energy likes a little fat! For a vegetarian version, you can substitute some big, meaty Portabella mushrooms for the steaks (baste with a little oil and watch carefully on the grill) and use vegetable instead of chicken broth. For the purest taste of flame, use mesquite charcoal and a fluid-free lighter in a covered grill. If you're using the broiler, position the rack 4 to 6 inches (10 to 15 cm) from the heat. To make the sauce in advance, prepare through step 3 and leave at room temperature for up to several hours before continuing.

Complements

Sip a red wine alongside, perhaps the one you used in the sauce. For a very yang meal, finish with Black Brownies.

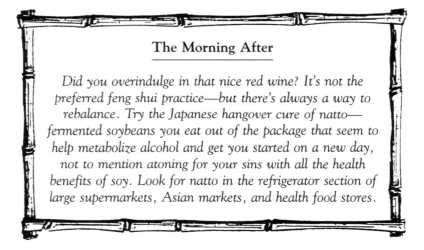

The Morning After

Did you overindulge in that nice red wine? It's not the preferred feng shui practice—but there's always a way to rebalance. Try the Japanese hangover cure of natto—fermented soybeans you eat out of the package that seem to help metabolize alcohol and get you started on a new day, not to mention atoning for your sins with all the health benefits of soy. Look for natto in the refrigerator section of large supermarkets, Asian markets, and health food stores.

The Feng Shui Plate

To experience the red Fire in this dish, cut each steak into slices. Spoon the mushrooms onto the top of the plate, arrange the slices on top, and drizzle any remaining sauce over. Serve the green-flecked white potatoes on the left to activate Wood (family and health, loyalty and forgiveness), or on the right to activate Metal (children, principles).

FIVE-ELEMENT PEANUT NOODLES Balanced

- 1 red pepper, julienned
- 1 yellow pepper, julienned
- 2 cups (500 ml) broccoli florets (about ½ head)
- 12 ounces (340 g) fresh Asian noodles (Chinese egg noodles or mein, Japanese yaki-soba, etc.)
- ½ cup (125 ml) canned sliced water chestnuts, rinsed and drained
- 2 scallions, sliced

The Peanut Sauce
- ½ cup (125 ml) creamy peanut butter
- 1 tablespoon minced garlic
- 1 tablespoon minced fresh ginger
- 1 serrano chili pepper, seeded and minced
- 1½ teaspoons sugar
- ½ teaspoon salt
- 2 tablespoons soy sauce
- ¼ cup (60 ml) rice vinegar
- ½ cup (60 ml) hot water
- 2 tablespoons sesame oil
- ½–1 teaspoon chili oil (see recipe on page 73, or purchase in the Asian section of the supermarket)

1. Bring a large pot of water to a boil. Using a pasta basket, if you have one, add the peppers and broccoli and blanch until just tender, about 4 minutes. Remove with the pasta basket or a slotted spoon, drain, and rinse thoroughly under cold water to stop the cooking.

2. Add the noodles to the boiling water and cook until they rise to the top and are just past al dente, about 3 minutes. Drain, rinse with cold water, and toss with a little sesame oil. Refrigerate the noodles and vegetables until serving time.

3. For the sauce, stir together the peanut butter, garlic, ginger, serrano pepper, sugar, salt, soy sauce, and vinegar. Add the hot water and stir until smooth, then gradually stir in the sesame oil and chili oil to taste. Set aside at room temperature to blend the flavors for up to several hours; if you're making farther in advance, chill and return to room temperature before serving.

4. To serve, toss the chilled noodles with 1/2 sauce and arrange on plates. Top with the blanched vegetables and water chestnuts, pour the remaining dressing over, and garnish with the scallions.

Serves 4.

The Essence of the Dish

This recipe balances the pure crunch of vegetables, tender bite of noodles, and richness of peanut sauce for a dish that is dense and satisfying, yet vegetarian and low in saturated fat. The peppers, broccoli, and water chestnuts represent the colors of Wood, Fire, Metal, and Earth, while a robust salty flavor contributes Water. Enjoy the Five-Element harmony of this recipe when you seek a model of balance to emulate or want to prolong a moment of equilibrium in your life. Chinese noodles (the world's first pasta) are a symbol of longevity, so look for the longest ones you can find!

Options and Opportunities

You can vary the recipe with an Indonesian twist by substituting the peanut sauce in the Lamb Satay recipe on page 143. You might try asparagus instead of broccoli and cucumber instead of water chestnuts.

Complements

This rich dish needs few additions, but you can cap the theme of balance with a spectacular finale of Fire and Ice Sundaes.

The Feng Shui Plate

Symbolize the complete confluence of the Five Elements by mixing the vegetables and scattering them over the noodles or emphasize their properties by placing the broccoli on the left, the red peppers at the top, the water chestnuts on the right, and the yellow peppers in the center.

FLEXIBLE STIR-FRY

Balanced

- 4 tablespoons soy sauce, divided
- 1 tablespoon sherry or Shaoxing rice wine
- 1 tablespoon cornstarch
- 1 teaspoon roasted sesame oil
- 1 tablespoon minced garlic
- 1 tablespoon minced fresh ginger
- ½ pound (225 g) boneless skinless chicken breast meat, cut in ½″ (1.25 cm) cubes *(and/or pork, beef, shrimp, tofu)*
- 2 cups (500 ml) napa cabbage, sliced thin (about ¼ head) *(and/or bok choy, broccoli, cauliflower)*
- 1 carrot, peeled and sliced thin *(and/or celery)*
- 1 red bell pepper, julienned *(and/or summer squash, water chestnuts, bean sprouts)*
- 1 cup sliced mushrooms, shiitakes or cultivated (about 2 ounces, or 65 g)
- 1 cup Chinese pea pods (about 3 ounces, or 85 g), ends snapped off and strings pulled *(and/or fresh or frozen and thawed peas)*
- 4 scallions, sliced
- 2 tablespoons peanut oil
- 3 cups (750 ml) cooked rice of your choice *(or cooked noodles)*

1. In a shallow dish, mix together 1 tablespoon of the soy sauce, the sherry, cornstarch, sesame oil, garlic, and ginger. Add the chicken, combine well, and set aside to marinate while you prepare the vegetables.
2. Group the vegetables together as follows: a) napa cabbage and carrots, b) pepper, mushrooms, and pea pods, c) scallions.
3. Place a wok or large skillet over high heat until very hot, add the peanut oil, and give it a few seconds to heat up. Add the ingredients in the following order at the intervals specified, stirring constantly:

a) The chicken with its marinade, about 1½ minutes, until no longer pink on the outside.
b) The cabbage and carrots, about 1½ minutes; the cabbage should be slightly softened.
c) The peppers, mushrooms, and pea pods, about 2 minutes, or until the mushrooms are just tender.
d) The scallions, 1 minute.
e) The remaining 3 tablespoons soy sauce, 1 minute.

4. Serve over hot rice.

Serves 4.

The Essence of the Dish

A stir-fry embodies the healthful Chinese aesthetic of balance and variety. Marrying yang meat with yin vegetables on a snowy white bed of neutral rice, it offers the proportions of protein, carbohydrates, fiber, and vitamins and minerals that have been shown to fuel health and energy.

The vegetables called for in the basic recipe cover the feng shui spectrum—green pea pods and scallions for Wood, red peppers for Fire, orange carrots for Earth, white rice and cabbage for Metal, black soy sauce and mushrooms for Water. There are also some nutritional superstars. The phytochemicals in carrots, cabbage, and peppers are associated with reduced risk of cancer and heart disease, and mushrooms are known as immune boosters.

You can rebalance the elemental mix with your own variations, adding ingredients that offer the elemental powers you need today.

Options and Opportunities

A good stir-fry is flexible, meaning that it can adapt to what you have on hand and what you like to eat. This recipe is designed for variation, allowing you to substitute or add ingredients to suit what's fresh in the market, what's available in your refrigerator, or what you crave today. Simply stick to the groupings and timings indicated above so that harder vegetables have a chance to cook a little longer and delicate ones don't turn to mush. If you choose broccoli or cauliflower and like it less crisp, you can blanch it in boiling water first.

If you'd rather use leftover cooked meat, add it in step d with the scallions. Mix up the marinade separately and add it with step c. Tofu will benefit if you press out the excess water before cutting it into cubes and marinating (see page 114).

To julienne peppers, halve and seed them, then cut them into quarters vertically along their natural veins. Cut each quarter into thin crosswise strips.

By the last step of the stir-fry, the vegetables should have given off enough natural juices to act as a sauce. If not, you can add a little chicken or vegetable stock to make sure the mixture moistens the rice. Some people like to drizzle fresh sesame oil over the finished plate.

Complements
A stir-fry covers all the bases. Finish with some Hot and Sour Mangoes and give yourself a hand for a healthful meal.

The Feng Shui Plate
Flexible Stir-Fry should occupy the whole plate, a mixed image of life's many colors, textures, flavors, and meanings working together to form a whole.

Rice Is Ready

In China, the phrase rice is ready *means dinner is served, indicating the fluffy grain's position at the heart of the meal. Though rice is now a staple around the world, China is thought to be its birthplace, and the subject is serious within these culinary circles.*

Though the Chinese were the first to discover that hulling the bran off rice can lead to vitamin deficiency and thus initiated the history of research in deficiency diseases, they nevertheless insist upon white rice for its perfect purity. Serving brown rice ups the vitamin and fiber content but muddies the image of pure white on your plate. With a world of rice now available across the country—basmati, jasmine, short-grain sticky rice, and more—you can explore the nuances of this ancient staple in endless permutations.

To cook long-grain white rice, rinse it and cover it with water to the depth of 1 inch (2.5 cm) above the top of the rice (if your fingers are the right length, you can use your knuckle as a gauge). Bring to a boil, stir, and reduce to a simmer. Cover and cook until tender and the liquid is absorbed, about 15 minutes. Fluff with a fork. You can expect the rice to approximately triple in volume while it cooks.

GRAPEFRUIT-POACHED SOLE
WITH WATERCRESS SAUCE

Yin

1   bunch watercress, tough stems removed
½   cup (120 ml) plus 2 tablespoons sour cream
2   tablespoons mayonnaise
1   shallot, minced
½   teaspoon Dijon mustard
¼   teaspoon salt
    Freshly ground black pepper
1   tablespoon olive oil
4   6-ounce (170 g) sole fillets
¾   cup (180 ml) fresh grapefruit juice (from 1 grapefruit)

1. To make the sauce, mince enough of the watercress leaves to make 1 tablespoon. Combine with the sour cream, mayonnaise, shallot, mustard, salt, and pepper and stir. Cover and chill until ready to serve.
2. Toss the remaining watercress with the olive oil and salt and pepper to taste. Set aside.
3. Season both sides of the sole with salt and pepper to taste and arrange in a wide skillet. Pour the grapefruit juice over the fish and marinate for 10 to 15 minutes.
4. Place the skillet over high heat just until the liquid starts to bubble, then immediately reduce the heat to low and poach until the fish flakes with a fork, about 1 minute per side.
5. To serve, arrange the watercress salad on plates, place the fish on top, and spoon just a little of the poaching liquid over to moisten. Top with the watercress sauce.

Serves 4.

The Essence of the Dish

Sole may be the most delicate of all fish, with a sweet flavor and custardy texture unmatched on land or sea. The more slow-moving and white-fleshed the fish, the more yin it is in

Fish: Good Fortune and Brain Food

In the Chinese tradition, fish symbolize success and abundance, which partly explains the popularity of fish tanks in the dining rooms of Chinese restaurants. Leaving a little fish uneaten on the plate represents having something left over after the necessities have been taken care of (and is also a diet trick many people swear by). The Chinese hang fish figures on their doors on New Year's Eve to elicit a prosperous year.

Not only do fish represent good fortune, but they're also considered brain food. There's good reason for this: Fish is rich in protein, which stimulates the production of norepinephrine, an alertness chemical in the brain. And perhaps clearer thinking brings on better luck!

Slow-moving, white-fleshed fish such as sole and flounder are considered yin, while active fish with red meat such as tuna, salmon, and swordfish are yang.

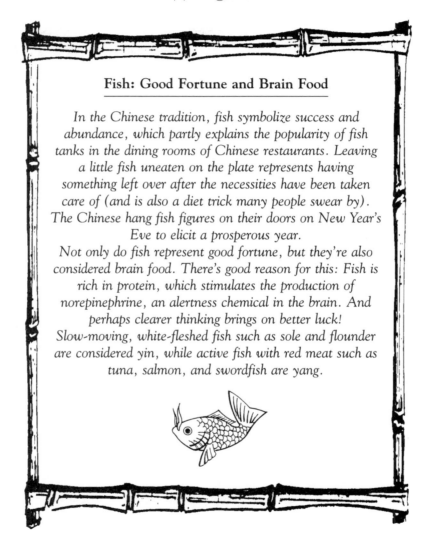

nature, and here slow, white sole combines with the cool energy of watercress and grapefruit (both anticarcinogenic foods) for a soothing dish that's subtle and rich.

With Wood energy from the green watercress and sour grapefruit, and complementary Fire in the watercress's bite, Grapefruit-Poached Sole is cleansing and good for circulation—a refreshing detox when you feel hot and cloudy.

Options and Opportunities

The dish is also delicious and even more yin when served cold. Let any leftovers make a quick and de-stressing lunch tomorrow.

Complements

This salad and entrée in one becomes a meal with the addition of just a simple first course or dessert. For a fresh and purifying meal during the dog days of summer—or their psychological equivalent—start with a first course of Green Grape Gazpacho or finish with Berry Balsamic Parfaits.

The Feng Shui Plate

To activate the elements, arrange the watercress over the upper left side of the plate, touching Wood and Fire to reinforce its green color and bitter taste. Overlap the sole slightly in the middle and stretch it out toward white Metal on the right side.

GRILLED TOFU SANDWICH
(A BETTER BURGER)

Balanced

2   14-ounce (400 g) blocks regular tofu, well pressed, or firm tofu, lightly pressed (see page 115)
1   tablespoon minced garlic
1   tablespoon minced fresh ginger
1   scallion, minced
¼   cup (60 ml) soy sauce
2   tablespoons sherry or Shaoxing rice wine
1   tablespoon rice vinegar
2   tablespoons roasted sesame oil
12 slices bread or 6 hamburger buns
     Your favorite sandwich or burger fixings—tomato, onion, lettuce, avocado, sprouts, mustard, mayonnaise, etc.

1. Cut each block of tofu into 8 slices about 1/2 inch (1.25 cm) thick. Arrange in a wide, nonreactive dish.
2. Combine the garlic, ginger, scallion, soy sauce, sherry, vinegar, and sesame oil and pour over the tofu. Marinate for at least 30 minutes or overnight, covered, in the refrigerator.
3. To grill: Preheat the grill or broiler. Remove the tofu from the marinade and grill or broil, 4 to 6 inches (10 to 15 cm) from the heat, until browned, about 3 to 5 minutes per side.
4. Serve on bread or buns with garnishes of your choice.

    Serves 6.

The Essence of the Dish

Some of a body's worst enemies present themselves between slices of bread or inside a bun, and the Grilled Tofu Sandwich puts a tasty stop to this sabotage. With superfood tofu standing in for processed cold cuts or high-fat hamburger, your qi flourishes as your immune system rearms. The tender, giving essence of yin tofu meets the yang energy of strong flavors and high-heat cooking within the neutral embrace of bread for the perfect balance of inside and outside that we know as the sandwich. A sandwich only works when the outer contains but doesn't dominate the inner; this is the balancing principle to contemplate as you smack your lips.

Options and Opportunities

Grilling gives this sandwich that irreplaceable taste of the flame. However, you might want to try a baked version, too, for a deep flavor and deliciously velvet-but-firm texture. To bake: Preheat the oven to 375° F (190° C). Bake the tofu in its marinade, turning every 10 minutes, until the tofu is browned and the marinade is mostly absorbed, about 40 minutes. There's no need to premarinate the tofu with this method, since it will absorb the marinade while it bakes.

Firm tofu is less likely to fall apart on the grill, but you can get away with well-pressed regular tofu, for better texture and flavor, if you bake it. Either way, the tofu tastes good cold, too, so make some extra to serve in sandwiches throughout the week.

For a chewier texture, try freezing your precut slices first.

If you're feeling very fat conscious, you can reduce or eliminate the oil in the marinade. For an even simpler tofu sandwich, substitute barbecue sauce for the marinade. Follow the same instructions for grilling or baking.

For a more traditional dish, serve the tofu with steamed rice and vegetables. Or buck tradition by using it anywhere you might expect to see meat or cheese, from chopped salad to pasta to your favorite soup or stew.

Complements

One of the reasons for the sandwich's abiding popularity is its self-contained nature. If you want more, sway your meal toward the yang with a summer picnic finish of Black Brownies, or wind down toward yin with Banana Coconut Cream Pudding.

LAMB SATAY WITH PEANUT SAUCE

Yang

1½ pounds (675 g) lamb sirloin, trimmed of fat and cut into ¾″ (2 cm) cubes

The Marinade
1 tablespoon minced fresh ginger
2 cloves garlic, minced
1 teaspoon ground coriander
2 tablespoons soy sauce
2 tablespoons fresh lime juice
1 tablespoon light brown sugar
½ teaspoon Asian chili sauce
2 tablespoons peanut oil

The Peanut Sauce
2 tablespoons peanut oil
1 tablespoon minced fresh ginger
3 cloves garlic, minced
2 shallots, minced
¼ cup (60 ml) canned coconut milk
½ cup (125 ml) creamy peanut butter
¼ cup (60 ml) water
2 tablespoons fish sauce
2 tablespoons light brown sugar
   Pinch cayenne pepper, or to taste
2 tablespoons (30 ml) fresh lime juice
   Chopped cilantro or basil, optional garnish

1. Combine all the marinade ingredients in a nonreactive dish or resealable plastic bag. Add the lamb cubes, combine well, cover or seal, and refrigerate overnight.

2. For the Peanut Sauce, heat the peanut oil in a medium saucepan over medium heat. Add the ginger, garlic, and shallots and sauté until soft but not browned, about 5 minutes.

3. Stir in the coconut milk, peanut butter, water, fish sauce, brown sugar, and cayenne and cook, stirring, for 5 minutes more.

4. Remove from the heat and transfer to a food processor. Add the lime juice and process until smooth. Adjust the seasonings to taste. Set aside at room temperature or, if you're making more than several hours in advance, refrigerate and bring to room temperature before serving.

5. Soak 12 wooden skewers in water for at least an hour.

6. Light the grill or place a rack about 4 inches (10 cm) from the broiler and preheat.

7. Thread the lamb cubes onto the skewers, leaving a little space between to allow for even browning. Grill or broil, basting with the marinade and turning once, until brown and just cooked through, about 2 to 3 minutes per side.

8. Serve with the Peanut Sauce for dipping. If you like, sprinkle with the optional herbs for garnish.

Serves 4.

The Essence of the Dish

The Chinese character for beauty is composed of the characters for lamb and big; apparently, the more lamb you eat, the more beautiful you become. The browned color and sweetness in the marinade and sauce invest this dish with Earth energy, so eat it when you want to be beautiful, warm, and expansive, or as an antidote to procrastination.

Options and Opportunities

You can substitute beef, pork, chicken, or shrimp for the lamb. Marinate shrimp for 1 to 2 hours; chicken can marinate for a few hours or up to overnight. If you're short on marinating time, skip the refrigerator and let the meat sit for 1 hour at room temperature while you make the sauce and set the table.

The sauce is quite rich and makes an ample amount for dipping. Serve leftovers later in the week with noodles or tossed with cooked vegetables; you might want to thin it with some hot water first.

Complements
You can also serve this satay as an appetizer (serves about 12; double the number of skewers), perhaps with White-Hot Cabbage Slaw for a yang meal of complementary elements (Earth and Metal) or with Stuffed Butternut Squash for a yin-yang Earth experience.

The Feng Shui Plate
Make a triangle of the skewers in the middle of the plate and put a dollop of Peanut Sauce in the center.

MENDING MOUSSAKA   Yang-Autumn

  2   medium eggplants, about 2 pounds (900 g) total, cut into ½" (1.25 cm) slices

The Filling
  2   tablespoons olive oil
  2   onions, chopped
12   ounces (340 g) mushrooms, sliced
  2   pounds (900 g) ground lamb
  2   cloves garlic, minced
  ¼   cup (60 ml) tomato paste
  ¼   cup (60 ml) dry red wine
  1   bay leaf
  2   teaspoons ground cinnamon
  2   teaspoons dried oregano
  ¼   cup (60 ml) chopped Italian parsley
  ¼   teaspoon salt
     Freshly ground pepper

The Custard
  ¼   cup (½ stick) unsalted butter
  ¼   cup (60 ml) unsifted flour
2½   cups (625 ml) hot milk
  2   egg yolks
  ½   teaspoon salt
  ¼   teaspoon nutmeg
     Dash white pepper

  4   ounces (120 g) feta cheese, crumbled

1. Preheat the oven to 375°F (190° C). Arrange the eggplant slices on a large, lightly oiled baking sheet, season with salt, cover with aluminum foil, and bake for 45 minutes. Remove and set aside, covered, to steam. Leave the oven on.
2. To make the filling, heat the olive oil in a large skillet over medium-high heat. Add the onions and mushrooms and sauté until the mushrooms are tender, 5 to 10 minutes. Add the lamb and garlic, turn up the heat, and sauté until the meat is just cooked through. Drain the fat, reduce the heat, and add the tomato paste, wine, bay leaf, cinnamon, oregano, parsley, salt, and pepper. Simmer until the liquid is absorbed, 5 to 10 minutes. Remove from the heat, remove the bay leaf, and set aside.
3. For the custard, melt the butter in a saucepan over medium heat. When it bubbles, whisk in the flour and cook, stirring constantly, for 2 minutes. Gradually whisk in the hot milk, thoroughly incorporating each addition before the next. Cook the sauce, whisking frequently, until thickened, about 5 minutes. Remove from the heat and let it cool, then whisk in the egg yolks, salt, nutmeg, and white pepper.
4. To assemble, oil a 9 × 13-inch (23 × 33 cm) baking dish and cover the bottom with 1/2 the eggplant slices. Top with 1/2 the filling and repeat. Pour the custard over all and sprinkle with the cheese. Bake, covered, for 45 minutes at 375°F (190° C). Uncover and continue baking until bubbling and lightly browned, about 15 minutes more. Let stand for 10 minutes before serving.

Serves 8.

The Essence of the Dish

Lamb is traditionally served on the first day of autumn in China to bring good fortune and start the process of "mending." It's also the meat of Fire, and its mending flame will stoke you up for the winter to come. Combining lamb with the downward-moving mushrooms and eggplant, the dish settles your qi from its summer heights and braces you for the seasonal transition into dormancy. Eggplant is also thought to enrich and move blood and strengthen the kidney and liver; meanwhile, the spices, the rich lamb, and the custard heat you from the inside out. This hearty casserole will warm and perfume your house and feed a group whose appetites are sharpened by crisp fall air.

Options and Opportunities

Italian brown field mushrooms are nice in this dish—or splurge by using part or all wild mushrooms.

Make a vegetarian version of Mending Moussaka by omitting the lamb and increasing the mushrooms to 2 pounds (900 g). You might want to double the amount of cheese for added protein and substance.

Complements

A warm spinach salad adds another downward-moving food to your fall meal.

The Feng Shui Plate

Let Fire's force enhance the downward movement of your qi by serving Mending Moussaka at the top of the plate. Arrange the spinach salad from the center out to Wood's left-hand gua.

MISO EGGPLANT   Yin

    1   pound (450 g) Japanese eggplants (about 4)
   2½   cups (625 ml) water, divided
    ¼   cup (60 ml) yellow miso paste
    2   tablespoons sugar
    2   tablespoons soy sauce
    3   tablespoons peanut oil
    1   teaspoon minced fresh ginger
    1   each green and red bell peppers, halved lengthwise, seeded, and cut into 1″ (2.5 cm)
         squares

1. Cut the eggplant crosswise into 1-inch (2.5 cm) lengths, then lengthwise into quarters. Cut 2 crosswise slits in the skin of each wedge. Place the eggplant in a bowl, cover with 2 cups (500 ml) of the water, and let stand for 5 minutes. Drain and pat dry.
2. In a small bowl, mix the miso with the sugar until smooth. Stir in the soy sauce, then the remaining 1/2 cup (125 ml) water.
3. Heat a wok or large skillet over high heat and add the oil. When the oil is hot, add the ginger and stir once. Add the eggplant and peppers and stir-fry for 5 minutes.
4. Add the miso mixture, reduce the heat, cover, and cook at a low boil, stirring occasionally, until the vegetables are tender, 10 to 15 minutes. Uncover, raise the heat, and cook and stir until the sauce is thickened and almost absorbed. Serve at once.

Serves 4 as a side dish or 2 as an entrée with rice.

The Essence of the Dish

Miso Eggplant has been known to win fans even among opponents of the vegetable. The caramelized sauce brings out the velvet texture of the soft, female eggplant, and a boost from thick, tangy miso paste makes this a satisfying vegetarian dish. The dark skin of the

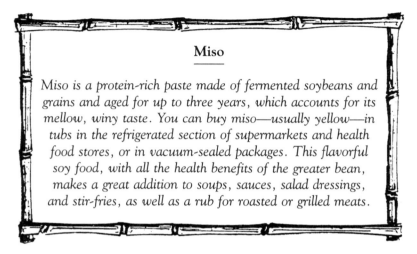

Miso

Miso is a protein-rich paste made of fermented soybeans and grains and aged for up to three years, which accounts for its mellow, winy taste. You can buy miso—usually yellow—in tubs in the refrigerated section of supermarkets and health food stores, or in vacuum-sealed packages. This flavorful soy food, with all the health benefits of the greater bean, makes a great addition to soups, sauces, salad dressings, and stir-fries, as well as a rub for roasted or grilled meats.

eggplants and salty sauce feed your Water energy to conjure up the midnight hour and the deep, innate understanding you feel at the very end of the day. Sweet yellow miso adds Earth, the green pepper Wood, and the red pepper Fire for a creative elemental mix.

Options and Opportunities
Soaking the eggplants in water helps prevent them from soaking up too much liquid from your stir-fry, so it's worth the extra step.

Complements
Add some steamed rice to round out the meal and complete the productive cycle with Metal.

The Feng Shui Plate
Make a mound of rice in Metal's gua on the right side of a small plate and fan the eggplant out into the remaining guas.

Mu Shu Chicken Wrap

Balanced

- 2 dried shiitake mushrooms
- 1 tablespoon soy sauce
- 1 tablespoon sherry or Shaoxing rice wine
- ½ teaspoon cornstarch
- 3 ounces (85 g) boneless skinless chicken breast meat, cut into matchsticks
- 1 large clove garlic, minced
- ½ teaspoon minced fresh ginger
- 1 teaspoon water
- ½ teaspoon roasted sesame oil
- ¼ carrot, peeled and shredded
- ¼ cup (60 ml) canned bamboo shoots, rinsed, drained, and cut into matchsticks
- ¼ cup (60 ml) chicken broth
- ¼ cup (60 ml) bean sprouts
- 1 scallion, cut into 1½" (3.75 cm) slivers
- 2 teaspoons peanut oil
- 1 flour tortilla
- 2 teaspoons hoisin sauce

1. Cover the dried shiitakes with hot water and soak for 30 minutes. Drain, stem, and slice.
2. Mix together the soy sauce, sherry, and cornstarch. Mix 1 tablespoon of this with the chicken, garlic, and ginger, and set aside to marinate while you prepare the vegetables. To the remaining mixture add the water and sesame oil; reserve.
3. Place a wok or large skillet over high heat until hot. Add the peanut oil and give it a few seconds to heat up. Add the chicken mixture and stir-fry until no longer pink on the outside, about 1 minute. Add the mushroom, carrot, bamboo shoots, and chicken stock, and cook for 2 minutes more. Add the bean sprouts and scallion and cook for

1 minute. Add the cornstarch mixture and cook, stirring, until the sauce thickens, about 1 minute more.

4. Spread the tortilla with the hoisin sauce and spoon the chicken mixture across the tortilla about 1/3 of the way up. Fold up the bottom edge, fold in the sides, and roll up.

Serves 1.

The Essence of the Dish

This self-contained dish for one is what to make when you're germinating a new idea. Inside the neutral white wrap lie all the flavors and colors of the Five Elements, hidden but potent like the roots of plants that haven't yet broken through the ground. Chicken and wheat combine to create the Wood energy of spring, reminding you that potential is often far greater than what is visible now. Make a Mu Shu Chicken Wrap, dine alone, and let what is within grow strong enough to emerge.

Options and Opportunities

For a classic variation on this dish, substitute pork loin for the chicken breast. Or go vegetarian by omitting the meat and increasing the vegetable proportions. Mix all the marinade together (everything in step 2) and add it with the bean sprouts and scallions.

Complements

Round out your meal and underscore Wood with a salad of cooked, chilled broccoli tossed in peanut oil with a squeeze of fresh lime juice.

The Feng Shui Plate

Serve the wrap all alone on the plate to reinforce the vision of bare springtime ground preparing to blossom.

ORANGE-BRAISED TOFU

Yin

½ cup (125 ml) water
¼ cup (60 ml) soy sauce
¾ cup (180 ml) fresh orange juice
2 tablespoons grated orange zest
2 tablespoons rice vinegar
2 tablespoons honey
½ teaspoon Chinese Five-Spice powder
¼ teaspoon salt
2 14-ounce (400 g) blocks firm tofu, halved horizontally

1. Combine all the ingredients but the tofu in a saucepan wide enough to hold the tofu in a single layer. Bring to a boil.
2. Add the tofu, reduce to a simmer, and cook for 15 minutes, turning the tofu halfway through. Remove from heat and cool the tofu in its liquid, turning a few more times. Cover and chill.

Serves 4.

The Essence of the Dish

Soft, sweet, and Earthy orange, this cool take on the greater bean moisturizes and nourishes your being like a good rain does a dry plant, slowing down your qi so that it can expand through your body and spirit. Its make-ahead and economical nature helps counter symptoms of Earth deficiency such as procrastination and miserliness, while its high protein count provides gentle strength to your cells. Earth's transitional energy makes this is a good get-back-on-track dish when your diet's been too rich, your schedule too swinging, or your thoughts too self-centered.

Options and Opportunities

Use two spatulas to turn the tofu cakes without breaking them, using the second one to brace the end as you scoop from underneath and then catch the cake as you flip. Braise the tofu when you bring it home from the store and keep it on hand for quick meals; the finished dish will last longer in your refrigerator than plain fresh tofu.

Complements

Try some mixed stir-fried vegetables alongside—snow peas, carrots, water chestnuts, mushrooms, and the like—for a delightful contrast of soft and crunchy, cold and hot. Or have a green salad tossed with peanut oil to coat and a spoonful of braising liquid. For a cool, Earth-orange meal packed with life-extending nutrients, start with a cup of Gingered Sweet Potato Soup.

The Feng Shui Plate

Serve the tofu in the center of the plate for Earth, drizzling some of the braising sauce over. Ring with vegetables or greens.

OYSTER EGG CUSTARD

Balanced-Spring

½	pound (225 g) shucked fresh oysters
2	tablespoons (¼ stick) unsalted butter, divided
1	onion, chopped fine
1	leek, white part only, chopped fine
1	carrot, chopped fine
1	stalk celery, chopped fine
1	clove garlic, minced
3	tablespoons dry white wine
8	eggs
2½	cups (600 ml) milk
2	tablespoons Parmesan cheese
¾	teaspoon salt
1	teaspoon curry powder
	White pepper

1. Preheat the oven to 350° F (177° C).
2. Drain the oysters, reserving any liquid. Melt 1 tablespoon of the butter in a skillet over medium-high heat, add the oysters, and sauté until plump and firm, about 2 to 3 minutes.
3. Season the oysters with salt and white pepper to taste and remove from the pan, leaving the liquid in the pan. Set the oysters aside.
4. Return the pan to medium heat and add the remaining tablespoon butter. Add the onion, leek, carrot, celery, and garlic and sauté until the onions are translucent, about 10 minutes. Add the white wine and stir to deglaze and evaporate the liquid. Remove from the heat and season with salt and white pepper to taste.
5. Coarsely chop the oysters.

6. In a medium bowl, whisk the eggs with a fork just until combined. Whisk in the reserved oyster liquid, any accumulated juices from the cooked oysters, the milk, Parmesan, salt, curry powder, and white pepper to taste.
7. Divide the vegetables evenly among 4 (2-cup, or 500 g, capacity) oven-proof bowls and top with the oysters. Pour the egg mixture over.
8. Place the bowls in a baking dish, place in the oven, and pour boiling water into the dish to the depth of 1 inch (2.5 cm). Bake until the custards are golden brown and set, about 35 to 40 minutes. Carefully remove the bowls from the pan and let them sit for 5 minutes. Serve the custards in the bowls set on plates.

Serves 4.

The Essence of the Dish

The egg is the ultimate symbol of the rebirth and fertility of spring, and here you enjoy its nuance in a delicate custard that prepares your qi for the season of renewal. Oysters, carrots, and celery all move upward like the growth of spring, elevating your qi from the subterranean depths of winter to reach toward the sun.

Oyster Egg Custard can also help you get spring fever of another kind. You've probably heard about the aphrodisiac qualities of oysters. Their zinc actually increases semen volume and blood testosterone levels for men and is essential to ovulation for women. So try this sensuous and effective concoction for a regenerative dinner à deux.

Options and Opportunities

If the vegetables start to stick as you sauté them, add just a little water, remembering that you'll deglaze the pan with wine at the end.

This recipe calls for full-size bowls, not custard cups. Be sure they're oven-proof!— and if they're wide, you'll probably need two baking dishes to hold them. It's best to warn everybody at the table that the bowls are hot. You can also serve the custard cold, a refreshing option on a warm spring day.

Don't delay your springtime celebration; April is the end of prime oyster season (months containing the letter r). You can substitute canned smoked oysters for a very different flavor and texture.

Complements

The custard's chameleon nature makes it work for breakfast, brunch, lunch, or dinner. For a morning meal, add toast points, orange juice, and tea. For lunch or dinner, try some chilled steamed asparagus drizzled with roasted sesame oil alongside, a baby green salad, or any other tender picks from the produce department, and a loaf of good bread. You can also make half portions in custard cups and serve them as a first course—perhaps with a Flexible Stir-Fry featuring the freshest spring vegetables, or a light pasta dish such as Broccoli Bowties.

Peppered Tuna With Wasabi Sauce   Yang

- 4   (6-ounce, or 170 g) ahi tuna steaks
      Salt
- 4   teaspoons cracked black pepper
      Oil

The Wasabi Sauce

- ½   cup (125 ml) rice wine vinegar
- 1   scallion, minced
- 1   teaspoon minced fresh ginger
- 4   teaspoons wasabi paste
- 2   tablespoons heavy cream
- 2   tablespoons soy sauce
- 6   tablespoons (¾ stick) unsalted butter, cut into pieces

1. Season both sides of each tuna steak with salt and sprinkle with the pepper, pressing it into the steaks. Refrigerate while you prepare the sauce.
2. To make the Wasabi Sauce, combine the vinegar, scallion, ginger, and wasabi in a small saucepan. Bring to a boil, reduce to a simmer, and cook until reduced by 1/2. Add the heavy cream and reduce by 1/2 again (it will be thick and green). Stir in the soy sauce and keep warm over lowest heat.
3. Place a large cast-iron skillet over high heat and coat the bottom with oil. When hot, sear the tuna, 1 minute on each side for rare. Remove to a plate and keep warm in the oven on the lowest setting.
4. To finish the sauce, whisk in the butter one piece at a time. Serve the tuna with the sauce.

Serves 4.

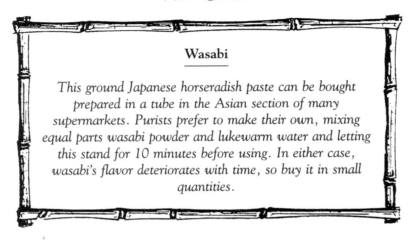

Wasabi

This ground Japanese horseradish paste can be bought prepared in a tube in the Asian section of many supermarkets. Purists prefer to make their own, mixing equal parts wasabi powder and lukewarm water and letting this stand for 10 minutes before using. In either case, wasabi's flavor deteriorates with time, so buy it in small quantities.

The Essence of the Dish

This dish burns with Fire in the red fish and bitter wasabi and pepper. Rounded out by a rich sauce likely to have you licking the plate, it will stimulate your circulatory system, banish lingering moisture, and strengthen your qi. Fire is the element of fame and wisdom, and this is a voluptuous dish to bring on or celebrate a very auspicious moment.

Options and Opportunities

Rare is the best way to cook this dish. The smoky black crust cloaks a tender steaklike interior that soaks up the sauce beautifully. If you can find a tuna loin (long and thin, like a pork tenderloin), it's even better for searing than the steaks. Work quickly and be careful not to overcook.

Complements

Try some sticky rice sprinkled with sesame seeds, and a salad of steamed snap peas and baby beets.

The Feng Shui Plate

Show off the rare tuna's red center by cutting it into slices, making a pool of sauce from the center of the plate up to Fire at the top, and overlapping the tuna slices on the sauce. If you're serving rice, put it on the right; the snap pea salad goes on the left to activate green Wood.

Pineapple-Ham-Stuffed Yam

Balanced

1   yam
2   teaspoons unsalted butter
1   teaspoon roasted sesame oil
1   teaspoon light brown sugar
½   cup (125 ml) canned crushed pineapple in juice
2   ounces (65 g) cooked ham, julienned
    Dash nutmeg
¼   teaspoon salt, or to taste
    Freshly ground pepper

1. Preheat the oven to 450° F (232° C). Prick the yam a few times with a fork and bake until soft, 45 to 50 minutes.
2. Remove the yam from the oven and let it sit until it's cool enough to handle. Cut in half and carefully scoop out the flesh, leaving the skin intact.
3. Place the yam flesh in a small bowl and mash it with a fork until it's very smooth. Mash in the butter, sesame oil, and brown sugar, then stir in the pineapple, ham, nutmeg, salt, and pepper.
4. Spoon the filling back into the yam skins and return to the oven. Bake until the skins are crisp, the yam is heated through, and you see flecks of golden brown on the top, 15 to 20 minutes.

Serves 1.

The Essence of the Dish

This easy-to-make take on a twice-baked potato delivers a healthful and satisfying meal for very little effort. And one sweet potato (which, in this country, is the same thing as a yam) has half your daily dose of vitamin E, an antioxidant that might help prevent heart disease.

That's seventy-six times as much as a white potato! Chinese medicine holds that yams supplement qi, strengthen the spleen and stomach, build tissue, and relieve weakness and fatigue.

This recipe resounds with the sweet, yellow energy of Earth. Try it when you're suffering from a bout of procrastination or selfishness.

Options and Opportunities

While a single yam makes a convenient no-leftovers dish for dining alone, you can easily multiply this recipe to feed a crowd. Try a vegetarian version with some chopped toasted walnuts instead of the ham.

Complements

The beauty of Pineapple-Ham-Stuffed Yam is that it's a perfect balance of carbohydrate, protein, vitamins, and fiber. There's no need to add a thing!

The Feng Shui Plate

Position your sweet potato in the center of your plate, and contemplate what you can do for the Earth as you feast upon its essence.

PORK AND SHRIMP WONTONS
WITH CILANTRO PESTO

Balanced

The Cilantro Pesto

¼ cup (60 ml) roasted peanuts
1 teaspoon chopped fresh ginger
2 cloves garlic, coarsely chopped
1 cup (250 ml) packed fresh cilantro leaves (about ¾ bunch)
2 tablespoons fresh lemon juice
½ teaspoon sugar
½ teaspoon salt
6 tablespoons peanut oil

The Wontons

½ pound (225 g) ground pork
¼ pound (120 g) raw shrimp, peeled and chopped
2 scallions, minced
1 egg white
1 tablespoon soy sauce
1½ teaspoons sherry or Shaoxing rice wine
1½ teaspoons cornstarch
¼ teaspoon salt
1 tablespoon water
½ pound (225 g) wonton wrappers (about 36)

1. For the Cilantro Pesto: Place the peanuts, ginger, and garlic in a food processor and grind to a paste. Add the cilantro leaves and blend until processed. Add the lemon juice, sugar, and salt and blend. With the machine running, slowly pour in the peanut oil. Set aside at room temperature to allow the flavors to blend.

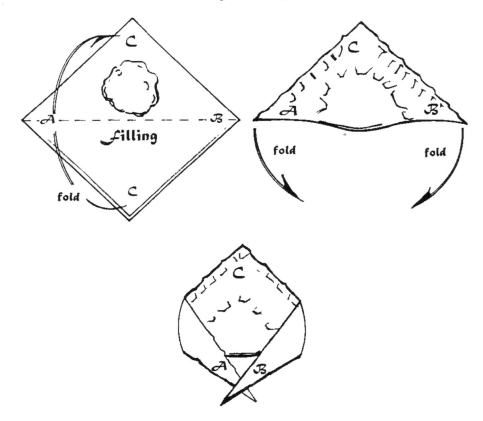

2. For the filling: Stir together the raw pork, shrimp, scallions, egg white, soy sauce, sherry, cornstarch, salt, and water. Refrigerate until you're ready to use.

3. To assemble the wontons: Have a small bowl of water on hand. Cover the unused wonton wrappers with a towel while you work to keep them from drying out. Place a wonton wrapper on your work surface with a corner facing you, like a diamond, and spoon a

teaspoon of filling into the center. Dip your finger in the water and moisten the top edges of the wrapper, then fold the bottom half up to meet them to form a triangle. Press the edges well to seal. Fold the bottom points of the triangle down in a V at the bottom of the wonton and pinch them together. Repeat with the remaining wontons and filling.

4. Bring a large pot of water to a boil and add the wontons. Cook until they float to the surface and the filling is cooked through, 3 to 5 minutes. Drain them carefully and serve drizzled with the Cilantro Pesto.

Serves 4 (about 36 wontons).

The Essence of the Dish

Creating and eating this dish is a meditative exercise. Several reiterative tasks—pulling cilantro leaves from their stems, peeling shrimp, stuffing wontons—are well suited for the Zen principle of practicing meditation during everyday tasks. Then, with the finished dish broadcasting Wood energy through the bright green and lemony pesto, you are perfectly positioned to ponder questions, weigh issues, and come to good decisions. Take on Pork and Shrimp Wontons when you have something to contemplate, or simply seek a feeling of meditative balance.

Options and Opportunities

The trick to this dish is learning to work with the wonton wrappers—but once you do, you'll be hooked on this versatile shortcut version of ravioli! Look for wonton wrappers in the refrigerated section of your supermarket (Dynasty is a common brand), or buy them at an Asian market. Resist the urge to overstuff them; this will only make it harder to seal the edges. Stuffed wontons can be frozen and cooked directly from the freezer; allow for a little extra cooking time. You can also forgo the pesto and serve the wontons in chicken broth with sliced scallions for a classic and balanced soup.

For the best flavor in the pesto, use a high-quality roasted peanut oil. You can also serve the pesto with cooked noodles for a simpler balanced dish (try it with the Soba Noodle Platter on page 181), on grilled meat or seafood for yang, or tossed with steamed or grilled vegetables for yin. Make a double batch of pesto to enjoy these variations throughout the week.

The Feng Shui Plate
With white wonton wrappers, a blush of pink peeking through from the filling, and green pesto sauce, this dish forms a mini productive cycle of Wood, Fire, and Metal. Arrange the wontons over the top semicircle of the plate to activate these guas.

QUICK CHICKPEA CURRY   Yang

1	tablespoon peanut oil
1	onion, chopped
1½	tablespoons curry powder, or more to taste
1	teaspoon ground cumin
¾	pound (340 g) ground turkey
3	cloves garlic, minced
1	15-ounce (425 g) can chickpeas, drained and rinsed
1	14½-ounce (412 g) can chopped tomatoes, undrained
1	10-ounce (280 g) package frozen spinach
½	cup (125 ml) chicken broth
½	teaspoon salt
	Optional garni: grated coconut, chopped peanuts, plain yogurt, chopped cilantro

1. Place the peanut oil in a saucepan over medium heat and sauté the onion, curry powder, and cumin until the onion is softened, about 5 minutes. Add the turkey and garlic, turn the heat up to medium high, and sauté until the turkey is just cooked through, about 5 minutes more.
2. Add the remaining ingredients (except optional garni), cover, raise the heat to high, and bring to a boil. Reduce the heat to medium and simmer, covered, stirring frequently to break up the spinach, for 15 minutes more.
3. Serve into bowls with accompaniments of your choice.

Serves 4.

The Essence of the Dish

Sometimes you need a good, hot yang meal with a minimum of shopping or prep work, and Quick Chickpea Curry provides this fast hit of heat. While the spices and turkey warm your qi, a full productive elemental cycle of Wood (turkey, spinach), Fire (tomatoes), Earth (curry), Metal (onion, chili), and Water (chickpeas) feeds your creative energy. Meanwhile, you get a good dose of vitamins, minerals, and fiber in a low-fat dish. It's impressively tasty and healthful—despite leaning on cans, the freezer, and premixed spices!

Options and Opportunities
Look for imported Indian or "Oriental" curry powder; these blends offer a much more interesting (and hotter) spice mix than the American kind. Experiment with the amount if you like things extra spicy.

For a vegetarian version, leave out the turkey and add a handful of cashews, which provide complementary protein to the chickpeas.

Complements
Add salad made with packaged mixed greens, maybe some frozen yogurt to cool down afterward—and you have a full meal with no fuss.

The Feng Shui Plate
The Five Elements naturally blend in the bowl—but if you choose to garnish, try some yogurt or coconut in Metal's right gua, peanuts in the center for Earth, and a sprinkle of cilantro to the left for Wood.

SAKE-GLAZED BLACK COD WITH PONZU RELISH Yang

½	cup (125 ml) sake
½	cup (125 ml) mirin (sweet Japanese cooking wine)
½	cup (125 ml) fresh orange juice
½	cup (125 ml) soy sauce
2	tablespoons sugar
1½	pounds (675 g) black cod fillets (skin on, if possible)
1	ear corn, kernels cut from the cob
4	Roma tomatoes, chopped
4	scallions, sliced
1	red or yellow pepper, diced
½	teaspoon minced fresh ginger
1	clove garlic, minced
½	cup (125 ml) chicken broth
	Salt and pepper to taste

1. Combine the sake, mirin, orange juice, soy sauce, and sugar in a saucepan. Bring to a boil, reduce the heat to medium high, and cook until reduced by 1/2, about 15 minutes. Cool.
2. Arrange the cod in a nonreactive dish. Reserve 1/4 cup (60 ml) of the marinade and pour the remainder over the fish. Cover and refrigerate overnight.
3. Close to serving time, combine all the vegetables with the reserved marinade and the chicken broth. Bring to a boil, reduce the heat to medium high, and boil gently until the liquid is almost absorbed, 10 to 15 minutes. Season to taste with salt and pepper and keep warm.
4. Prepare the grill or preheat the broiler with the rack 4 to 6 inches (10 to 15 cm) from the heat. Grill or broil the cod, skin side to the heat first, until browned, about 4 to 5 min-

utes. Turn, baste, and cook until browned and flaky, about 2 to 3 minutes. Serve with the vegetable relish.

Serves 4.

The Essence of the Dish
Seared, crispy, and caramelized, this dish has the energy of yang without the fat. In fact, at 2.4 grams of fat per serving, it's about as low as you can go. But cod, a favorite of the Japanese kitchen, is deceptively rich; its alternate name is butterfish, and it cooks up into thick, buttery flakes. The combination of the sweet marinade and the flavor of smoke makes this dish great for the summer barbecue, and a nice way to feed your yang in warm weather without weighing yourself down with heavier fare.

Options and Opportunities
The crisp skin is one of the pleasures of this dish, but some markets routinely skin their cod fillets. Skinless will do if it's all you can find.

Complements
Steam some rice while you make the relish. Continue the theme of low-fat yang by popping some fruit on the grill for an interesting dessert; drizzle with honey mixed with a hint of chopped fresh rosemary.

The Feng Shui Plate
Place the cod in the center for the Earth energy of its sweet marinade and brown glaze. Spoon the relish alongside, to the left if you want Wood's energy of loyalty, family, and health, or at the top for a dose of Fire's wisdom and fame.

Salt-Roasted Duckling With Beer-Braised Cabbage

Yang-Winter

- 4 cups (1 l) rock salt
- 1 4–5-pound (1,800–2,250 g) raw duckling, excess fat removed
- 3 cloves garlic, minced
- 1 teaspoon minced fresh ginger
- 1 tablespoon Chinese Five-Spice powder
- ½ teaspoon salt
  Freshly ground pepper

The Beer-Braised Cabbage

- 2 tablespoons (¼ stick) unsalted butter
- 1 large red onion, halved vertically and sliced thin lengthwise
- 8 ounces (225 g) red cabbage, shredded (about 5 cups, or 1.2 l)
- 1 bay leaf
- ½–1 teaspoon salt
  Freshly ground pepper
- 1 cooking apple, peeled, quartered, cored, and sliced crosswise
- ¾ cup (180 ml) beer
- ¾ cup (180 ml) chicken broth
- 2 tablespoons cider vinegar
- 2 tablespoons light brown sugar

1. Preheat the oven to 450° F (232° C) and spread the rock salt in a roasting pan. Remove the giblets and neck from the duckling and rinse it inside and out. Pat dry and, beginning at the leg end, use your hands to carefully loosen the skin from the breast and drumsticks. Use your fingers as probes to tear the connecting tissue.
2. Combine the garlic, ginger, Five-Spice powder, 1/2 teaspoon salt, and pepper and rub under the loosened skin and inside the body cavity. Truss the legs together with

kitchen string and place the duck, breast-side up, in the prepared roasting pan. Pierce the breast several times with a fork and roast until the duckling is plump, golden brown, and crispy, and a meat thermometer inserted into the meatiest part of the thigh registers 180°F (82° C), about 50 minutes. Remove from the oven and let it stand, loosely covered with foil, for 10 minutes before serving. Remove to a board and carve.

3. While the duck roasts, make the Beer-Braised Cabbage: Melt the butter in a large skillet over medium heat. Add the onion and sauté until softened, several minutes. Add the cabbage and toss, then add the bay leaf, salt, pepper, apple, beer, broth, vinegar, and brown sugar. Cover, raise the heat to high, and bring to a boil. Lower the heat and cook at a low boil, stirring occasionally, until everything is tender, about 7 to 12 minutes. Uncover and continue to cook until the liquid is mostly absorbed, 5 to 10 minutes more. Remove the bay leaf and adjust the salt and pepper to taste.

4. Serve the cabbage onto plates, top with the duckling, and drizzle any accumulated carving juices over the top.

Serves 4.

The Essence of the Dish

This hearty dish for winter will warm your kitchen and the coldest bones. The rock salt roasting bed does double duty, keeping the duck out of the fat as it cooks, and joining with the hops in the beer to exert inward force on your qi and move it to your body's core to wait out the long winter season. The fresh garlic and ginger fight off colds and flu at the literal level, while the number five in the Five-Spice powder promotes healthfulness by subtler means. This rich and spicy dish exudes yang heat to stoke your inner furnace, and represents all Five Flavors for good elemental balance.

Options and Opportunities

If you buy a frozen duck, be sure to thaw it completely in the refrigerator before proceeding. A mortar and pestle will enable you to pound the garlic-spice mixture into a paste for easier distribution under the skin. Have faith and fearless fingers as you loosen the skin! A few tears aren't fatal.

Pick up a package of preshredded cabbage to save yourself a step. To enrich the dish's flavor, simmer the chicken broth plus 1/4 cup (60 ml) water (to compensate for evaporation) with the duck giblets and neck for 15 minutes; skim and strain before using. As you slice the apple, drop it into the beer to prevent it from turning brown.

To carve the duck, work from the side closest to you. Remove that leg and both wings and set aside. Now cut down the center of the breastbone and, starting at the leg end and working toward yourself and the neck, remove the breast half. Turn the duck around and repeat. Slice the breast meat crosswise and the drumsticks vertically. Use the wings as garnish or reserve for another use. Should you eat that delicious skin or not? Crispy and flavored with the spice rub, it's a wonderful addition to this yang dish. It's also high in fat. You decide, based on your own energy needs at the moment.

Be sure to discard all that fat-soaked roasting salt!

Complements

This dish requires little accompaniment other than perhaps some dark, chewy bread. For a very yang meal in the same flavor groove, finish with Five-Spice Almond Cake—or take it easy with a dessert of fresh oranges or tangerines, which add vitamin C to your array of winter defenses.

The Feng Shui Plate

Arrange the cabbage across the top of the plate for red Fire, then prop slices of duckling along its central edge in Earth's gua.

SEARED SALMON WITH HORSERADISH BUTTER   Yang

The Horseradish Butter

3   tablespoons unsalted butter, slightly softened
1   tablespoon Dijon mustard
2   teaspoons prepared horseradish
¼   teaspoon black pepper
    Dash cayenne pepper
    Dash salt

4   (6-ounce, or 170 g) salmon fillets
    Oil

1. To make the Horseradish Butter, stir together the butter, mustard, horseradish, black pepper, cayenne pepper, and salt. If you like, you can roll this into a small log in plastic wrap. Chill until firm.
2. Season the salmon with salt and pepper. Place a large cast-iron skillet over high heat. When it's hot, add oil to coat and heat for a few seconds more. Add the salmon, skin-side down first, and reduce the heat to medium high. Sear for about 1/2 to 2 minutes per side for medium rare.
3. Serve the salmon with a pat of the Horseradish Butter.

    Serves 4.

The Essence of the Dish

Fast and forthright, Seared Salmon combines high heat with rich and pungent flavors to serve up yang in a hurry. Fire and Metal prevail in the pink-and-white color scheme and the bitter and spicy flavors of the Horseradish Butter, and this creates a good dish for mustering forces on a day when things have gone wrong. Let Fire's energy and the salmon's omega-3 oils feed your heart and stoke your circulation while Metal provides the kind of productive life energy that can turn around bad fortune and bring better luck.

Options and Opportunities
Searing the salmon until it has just turned opaque up the sides will yield a nice brown exterior with a juicy, medium-rare interior; adjust the cooking time for the thickness of your fillets. If you prefer, you can peel the skin from the fillets after you cook them—but the crispy texture from the searing and the concentration of omega-3 oils there makes the skin a worthwhile and tasty addition!

Complements
Accompany the salmon with baby bok choy, cut in half and sautéed over medium-high heat, cut-side down, in a mixture of butter and peanut oil. Cook until brown, flip, reduce the heat to medium, cover, and cook until tender. You can further Fire's power and complete a superfood meal with a starter of Lively Lentil Salad.

The Feng Shui Plate
Serve the salmon on a diagonal on the upper right side of the plate, spanning Fire's and Metal's guas. Arrange the green bok choy to the left to activate Wood.

SENSUOUS SQUAB

Yang

- 2 (1-pound, or 450 g) squabs
  Salt and pepper
- 3 tablespoons unsalted butter, divided
- 2 tablespoons brandy
- ¼ cup (60 ml) dry red wine
- ½ cup (125 ml) chicken broth
- 10 cured black olives (Niçoise, Kalamata, etc.), pitted and halved

1. Preheat the oven to 400° F (204° C). Remove the giblets from the squabs and season all over with salt and pepper.
2. Melt 1 tablespoon of the butter in an oven-proof skillet over medium-high heat. Add the squab and brown well on both sides, about 3 to 5 minutes per side. Transfer the pan to the oven and roast, breast-side up, until the squabs are medium rare, about 12 to 16 minutes. Transfer to a platter and tent with foil.
3. Lightly skim the liquid in the skillet. Return it to medium-high heat until bubbling, add the brandy, and stir to deglaze. Cook down to a syrup, a minute or two. Add the red wine, stir, and reduce it by 1/2, another minute or two. Add the broth and olives and reduce until lightly syrupy, 5 to 6 minutes. Remove from the heat and whisk in the remaining 2 tablespoons butter a little at a time.
4. Pour the sauce onto plates and top with the squab.

Serves 2.

The Essence of the Dish

Eating squabs, which are pigeons before they learn to fly, is associated with sexuality in China because of the birds' active erotic habits and the fact that the female pigeon pursues the male. Thought by the Chinese to increase male potency, squabs are often eaten by pubescent adolescents and aging men. This preparation adds a dark sauce and soft, suggestive olives. Because the sauce unleashes Water's energy to make you more sociable and attractive, let Sensuous Squab fuel your next romantic dinner.

Options and Opportunities
Squabs are available at poultry markets or by special order from many butchers. You can substitute Cornish game hens, but might not derive the same libidinous benefits. Baste the birds with pan juices a time or two while they roast for moister results. To carve the squabs, slice down the middle of the breastbone and then slice off each breast half. If you like, remove the legs and wings to serve alongside.

Complements
Cooked spaghetti squash, pulled into strands and sautéed in a little butter and olive oil, adds color to the plate and helps soak up the delicious sauce. Cap your erotic repast with Yin-Yang Butterfly Dessert.

The Feng Shui Plate
Nap the sauce down toward the bottom of the plate to activate Water's gua and place the squab over it. If you're comfortable with your dining companion and don't mind getting messy, you can serve the squabs whole and dismantle them at the table (use steak knives), daring to suck the bones. If you'd rather maintain proper table manners, carve the squabs before serving, slicing the breasts and arranging them in overlapping slices over the sauce with the legs alongside as a garnish.

SESAME PORK CELLOPHANE NOODLES Balanced

2–3 boneless center-cut pork loin chops (about ¾ pound, or 340 g, total)
 4 teaspoons toasted sesame seeds, divided
 4 tablespoons soy sauce, divided
 4 teaspoons sugar, divided
 1 tablespoon roasted sesame oil, divided
 4 cloves garlic, crushed
 ¼ teaspoon black pepper
 ¼ teaspoon chili oil (see recipe on page 73, or purchase in the Asian section of the supermarket)
 4 ounces (120 g) cellophane noodles
 1 egg, separated
 4 tablespoons peanut oil
 1 onion, halved lengthwise and sliced crosswise
  Salt
 1 red bell pepper, seeded and julienned
 1 carrot, julienned
 3 ounces (85 g) fresh shiitake mushrooms, stemmed and sliced
 6 ounces (170 g) fresh spinach, coarsely chopped

1. Freeze the pork for easier slicing, 30 to 40 minutes, until firm but not frozen.
2. Crush the sesame seeds in a mortar or spice grinder until partially ground.
3. Slice the pork across the grain 1/8 to 1/4 inch (.25 to .5 cm) thick, then cut into strips 1/8 to 1/4 inch wide. In a nonreactive dish combine 1 tablespoon of the sesame seeds, 2 tablespoons of the soy sauce, 1 tablespoon of the sugar, 1/2 tablespoon of the sesame oil, the garlic, and the pepper. Stir to combine, then add the pork and mix well. Set aside to marinate at room temperature for at least 15 minutes. Combine the remain-

ing sesame seeds, 2 tablespoons soy sauce, 1 teaspoon sugar, 1/2 tablespoon sesame oil, and the chili oil in a small bowl and set aside.

4. Bring a large pot of salted water to a boil. Remove from the heat and add the noodles. Let them soak for 15 minutes. Drain.

5. Lightly beat the egg white and yolk in separate bowls. Oil a small, nonstick skillet and place over medium heat for 1 minute. Add the egg white, tilting to distribute, and cook until set, 1 to 2 minutes. Remove, reduce the heat to low, and repeat with the egg yolk. Place over the egg white sheet, roll both up together, and cut crosswise into shreds.

6. Heat 1/2 tablespoon of the peanut oil in a wok or large skillet over medium heat. Add the onion and sauté until tender, about 4 minutes. Sprinkle with salt and remove to a large bowl. Repeat with each of the vegetables, adding 1/2 tablespoon oil and salt each time and transferring to the bowl. Finish with the pork and marinade, cooking just until done, about 2 minutes. Remove from the wok and add to the bowl.

7. Add the remaining tablespoon of oil to the wok. When it's hot, add the noodles and stir-fry for 1 minute. Stir the reserved soy sauce mixture and add to the noodles, stirring and cooking for 30 seconds more. Add the pork and vegetables to the noodles and toss until well combined and heated through, about 30 seconds. Serve at once, garnished with the egg shreds.

Serves 4.

The Essence of the Dish

Balancing the firm bite of pork with slippery filaments of bean threads and a gardenful of vegetables . . . sweet with salt . . . and the colors of all Five Elements, Sesame Pork Cellophane Noodles present a model of integration. The noodles are colorless and flavorless until they meet the ingredients they're cooked with. Then they become the essence of the dish itself, a medium to convey and distill the colors and flavors around them, clarifying chaos with the tender results.

Sometimes, it behooves us all to act as cellophane noodles.

Options and Opportunities

Look for cellophane noodles, also known as bean-thread noodles because they're made from the starch of the mung bean, in the Asian section of the supermarket, Asian markets, and natural food stores. A 6-ounce (170 g) bag of prewashed spinach saves you time and provides just the right amount for the recipe.

If you prefer to omit the pork for a vegetarian dish, use 6 to 8 ounces (170 to 225 g) of noodles, increase the quantity of vegetables as you like, and combine all the marinade and sauce ingredients in one bowl to add to the noodles during the stir-fry.

Complements

The last-minute nature of stir-frying advises against a first course, so follow the noodles with fruit or dessert.

The Feng Shui Plate

This dish is pretty served on a plate that picks up one of its elemental colors.

SOBA NOODLE PLATTER

Yin

12 ounces (340 g) dried soba noodles

The Dashi Dipping Sauce
2 cups (500 ml) water
½ tablespoon instant dashi (Japanese soup stock)
¼ cup (60 ml) soy sauce
¼ cup (60 ml) rice vinegar
¼ cup (60 ml) sugar
2 tablespoons sake
1 tablespoon grated orange zest

Accompaniments: grated daikon, mung bean sprouts, seeded julienned cucumber, sliced scallions

1. Bring a large pot of salted water to a boil, add the noodles, stir, and return to a boil. Add 1 cup (250 ml) cold water and return to a boil again. Remove from the heat and let stand for 5 minutes. Drain and rinse well, separating the noodles with your fingers. Spread on a clean dish towel and pat dry, cover, and chill.
2. For the Dashi Dipping Sauce, bring the water to a boil. Add the instant dashi and reduce to a simmer. When the dashi is dissolved, add the soy sauce, vinegar, sugar, and sake. Return to a simmer and cook for 2 minutes more. Remove from the heat, stir in the orange zest, cool, and chill.
3. To serve, place the chilled noodles in bowls (rinse with water and dry if they're stuck together). Arrange on big plates, along with small bowls containing the dipping sauce and piles of the accompaniments. Using chopsticks, grab noodles and accompaniments and dip each bite into sauce as desired.

Serves 4.

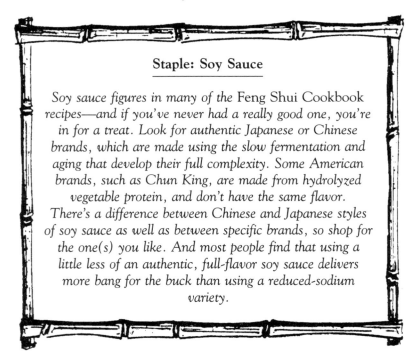

Staple: Soy Sauce

Soy sauce figures in many of the Feng Shui Cookbook recipes—and if you've never had a really good one, you're in for a treat. Look for authentic Japanese or Chinese brands, which are made using the slow fermentation and aging that develop their full complexity. Some American brands, such as Chun King, are made from hydrolyzed vegetable protein, and don't have the same flavor. There's a difference between Chinese and Japanese styles of soy sauce as well as between specific brands, so shop for the one(s) you like. And most people find that using a little less of an authentic, full-flavor soy sauce delivers more bang for the buck than using a reduced-sodium variety.

The Essence of the Dish

This classic Japanese noodle presentation teaches patience and grace. Designing each bite as you go and maneuvering noodles from bowl to sauce to mouth requires your full presence in the moment. All five flavors are here, and you can combine them in any permutations you like, exercising your ability to pinpoint your desires, sort out the variables, and execute a plan.

This dish is also fat-free. Now, isn't that refined?

Options and Opportunities

Soba noodles are Japanese noodles made from buckwheat; they're available in many supermarkets, Asian markets, and natural food stores. They can vary in thickness, so adjust the standing time as necessary. You can also make this dish with udon noodles, but you'll lose the nutty flavor and naturally high protein count of the buckwheat.

For a variation, serve the noodles with Cilantro Pesto (page 163) instead of or in addition to the Dashi Dipping Sauce. Thin the pesto with water to dipping consistency. You can also experiment with the accompaniments. Try grated carrot, matchsticks of jicama, or whatever you have on hand.

Make your noodles and sauce in advance so they have time to chill—and then appreciate the convenience of a complete make-ahead meal!

Complements

Half portions of Chilled Tofu With Scallions and Sesame Oil as a first course make for a relaxing, Zen-like meal that also happens to be nutritionally balanced and low in fat.

The Feng Shui Plate

You can activate all the elemental guas by putting the bowl of Earth-brown noodles in the center of the plate with the Dashi Dipping Sauce at the bottom, the scallions to the left, the daikon and cucumber at the top, and the bean sprouts to the right.

SPICY SESAME CHICKEN

Yang

¼ cup (60 ml) sesame seeds
1 teaspoon ground ginger
½ teaspoon anise seeds
½ teaspoon cayenne pepper or more to taste
⅛ teaspoon salt
  Freshly ground black pepper
4 boneless, skinless chicken breast halves (1 pound, or 450 g)
2 tablespoons soy sauce
2 teaspoons honey
2 teaspoons balsamic vinegar
3 tablespoons roasted sesame oil
2 teaspoons minced garlic

1. Combine the sesame seeds, ginger, anise, cayenne, salt, and black pepper in a shallow rimmed dish and lightly dredge the chicken in the mixture.
2. Combine the soy sauce, honey, and balsamic vinegar and set aside.
3. Heat the oil in a large skillet over medium-high heat. Add the chicken and cook until browned, 3 to 4 minutes. Reduce the heat to medium, flip, and cook the chicken until firm and cooked through, 3 to 4 minutes more. Remove the pan from the heat, transfer the chicken to a plate, and keep warm.
4. Add the garlic to the pan and stir. Return to the heat and cook until fragrant. Add the soy sauce mixture, stir to deglaze the pan, and cook until slightly thickened, a minute or two.
5. Serve the chicken onto plates and drizzle the pan juices over each.

   Serves 4.

The Essence of the Dish

Heat, salt, sweet, sour, and the bitterness of browned spice—Spicy Sesame Chicken covers all Five Elements while providing the stimulating energy of yang. The spicy coating also summons the energy of Metal, which provides the productive force to relieve stagnation in your life and help you take a chance. Try Spicy Sesame Chicken to accelerate your energy and breath when it's time to live a little faster.

Options and Opportunities

Lightly pounding the chicken breasts allows you to make them of uniform thickness so they cook at the same rate. There will be lots of sesame seeds in the pan when you remove the chicken; don't worry—they'll simply become part of the delicious sauce!

Crank up the cayenne pepper if you're seeking extra yang heat. If you're serving rice on the side, you can also double the deglazing sauce (garlic, soy sauce, honey, and balsamic vinegar) to drizzle over the top. A quick zap in the microwave will melt your honey for easier measuring.

Complements

Steamed rice and some sautéed green beans (try them in roasted sesame oil with a few drops of anisette) complement the flavors and elemental powers of Spicy Sesame Chicken.

The Feng Shui Plate

This black-sauced dish is happiest in Water's gua at the bottom of the plate. Put rice on the right for white Metal, and green beans on the left for Wood.

SQUID INK PASTA WITH CALAMARI AND SUMMER VEGETABLES

Balanced

6   ounces (170 g) dried squid ink pasta
5   tablespoons extra-virgin olive oil, divided
¾   pound (340 g) zucchini, julienned
1   yellow pepper, seeded and julienned
1   tablespoon minced garlic
1   tablespoon chopped Italian parsley
¾   pound (340 g) fresh calamari, cut into rings
½   cup (125 ml) dry white wine
2   Roma tomatoes, seeded and julienned
   Dash cayenne pepper
   Freshly grated Parmesan cheese
   Salt and pepper

1. Bring a large pot of water to a boil. Salt generously, return to a boil, and cook the pasta according to package directions.
2. Meanwhile, heat 2 tablespoons of the olive oil in a large skillet over high heat. Add the zucchini and pepper and sauté, stirring, just until tender. Season with salt and pepper, remove from the pan, and keep warm.
3. Return the pan to medium-high heat and add 1 tablespoon olive oil. Add the garlic and parsley and stir until fragrant and sizzling. Add the calamari and sauté for 1 minute. Add the wine and simmer for 2 minutes more, then add the tomatoes and cayenne and simmer until the tomatoes are just softened, about another minute. Remove from the heat and stir in 1 tablespoon olive oil, 2 tablespoons Parmesan cheese, and salt and pepper to taste.
4. Drain the pasta and toss with the squash, pepper, and 1 tablespoon olive oil. Serve onto warm plates and top with the calamari sauce, passing additional cheese at the table.

   Serves 4.

The Essence of the Dish

This striking pasta dish is not only beautiful, it's also a Five-Element palette on a plate. The squid, with its black ink and white flesh, is the ultimate yin-yang creature, and here the balance of black and white is supported by green, red, and yellow for a full productive cycle.

A quick, delicious, and healthful dish of pasta, vegetables, seafood, and olive oil is a good cooking habit for maintaining balance all your life. It contains everything you need, nourishing your senses and your cells without consuming too much precious time.

Options and Opportunities

This dish can be varied in many ways while still maintaining its Five-Element balance. Swap vegetables within the same color family—spinach instead of zucchini, julienned carrots instead of the yellow pepper, and so forth. You can make it vegetarian by substituting pressed tofu for the calamari. If you'd prefer to do without the wine, use fish or chicken stock or clam juice instead.

Complements

Add a green salad, and perhaps some sautéed pears or baked bananas for dessert.

The Feng Shui Plate

The black pasta and remaining elemental colors are set off best by big white plates.

STUFFED BUTTERNUT SQUASH   Yin

2 small (1-pound, or 450 g) butternut squash
Peanut oil
Salt and pepper
1 cup (250 ml) diced red bell pepper
½ cup (125 ml) sliced scallions
½ cup (125 ml) hulled millet
1½ cups (375 ml) chicken broth
½ cup (125 ml) corn kernels, fresh or frozen and thawed
2 tablespoons chopped Italian parsley
½ teaspoon salt
⅛ teaspoon pepper
2 tablespoons (¼ stick) unsalted butter
2 teaspoons roasted sesame oil

1. Preheat the oven to 350° F (177° C). Halve the squash lengthwise, remove the seeds and membranes, brush the 4 cut surfaces with some peanut oil, and season with salt and pepper. Place cut-sides down on a baking sheet and bake until tender and caramelized, about 45 minutes.
2. While the squash are baking, heat 1 tablespoon peanut oil in a large skillet over medium heat. Add the peppers and scallions and sauté for 2 minutes. Add the millet and sauté, stirring, until golden brown and starting to smell nutty, about 4 minutes more. Pour in the chicken broth, cover, and bring to a boil. Reduce the heat and simmer, covered, until the millet is tender and the liquid is absorbed, about 20 minutes. Remove from the heat and let stand for 10 minutes more. Fluff with a fork.
3. When the squash are done and cool enough to handle, scoop out the flesh, leaving the shells intact. Mash the pulp by hand or puree in a food processor.

4. Add the squash pulp, corn, parsley, salt, and pepper to the millet and combine thoroughly. Stuff back into the squash shells and place on a baking sheet.
5. Melt the butter and stir in the sesame oil. Drizzle over the squash. Bake at 350° F (177° C) until bubbling and golden brown, about 20 minutes.

Serves 4.

The Essence of the Dish
The first recorded mention of millet was in the Chinese agricultural guide *Fan Shen-Chiu Shu,* circa 2800 B.C., which declared it one of China's five sacred crops. A staple of ancient civilizations from the Greeks to the Visigoths and postulated to be a favorite snack of the dinosaurs, millet has been nourishing earth's creatures for millennia and remains an important food throughout the non-Western world—for good reason. Rich in B vitamins, iron, and calcium, millet also earns a high protein rating and is particularly strong in the immune-boosting amino acid lysine.

With such essential attributes, it's not surprising that millet is the grain of the element Earth, and here it joins with elemental mates scallions, butternut squash, and corn for a dish overflowing with nourishing, harmonizing Earth energy. Corn also complements millet for high-quality vegetable protein, so you can enjoy this vegetarian dish knowing all your needs have been met. Earth is the element of honesty; try sweet, sesame Stuffed Butternut Squash when you're having trouble telling someone the truth.

Options and Opportunities
Be sure to buy millet meant for people, not birds! It's available at natural food stores. If you bake the squash until they're very tender, the pulp will pop right out and you can eat the entire finished product, skin and all. Be extra careful not to tear the soft skins as you scoop.

Complements
Finish your meal with the Earthiest of fruits, apricots.

The Feng Shui Plate
The center of the plate is the only spot for this Earth-infused dish.

SUSHI-STYLE SALMON TARTARE   Yin

1½ pounds (675 g) fresh salmon fillets
2   scallions, minced
¼   cup minced pickled ginger (about 2 ounces, or 60 ml), plus additional for garnish
2   teaspoons prepared wasabi, plus additional for garnish
1   tablespoon fresh lime juice
1   tablespoon roasted sesame oil
½   teaspoon salt, or to taste
    Freshly ground black pepper
4   sheets nori (Japanese seaweed)

1. Cut the skin from the salmon and roughly dice the fish. Pulse in the food processor just until minced. Do not overprocess.
2. Transfer the salmon to a bowl and add the scallions, pickled ginger, wasabi, lime juice, sesame oil, salt, and pepper. Gently stir to combine. Cover and refrigerate until cold.
3. At serving time, place a large skillet over medium-high heat and toast each nori sheet until bright green, about 2 minutes per side. Cut each sheet into 4 squares, arrange on a plate, and top with the salmon tartare.

Serves 4 as an entrée or 8 as an appetizer.

The Essence of the Dish

This raw presentation is a good way to enjoy the richness of salmon while still enhancing your yin energy. The heart-healthy omega-3 oils in the fish combine with nori, rich in vitamins A and C, and the cardiovascular Fire energy of pink fish and bitter wasabi to make Sushi-Style Salmon Tartare good for long life.

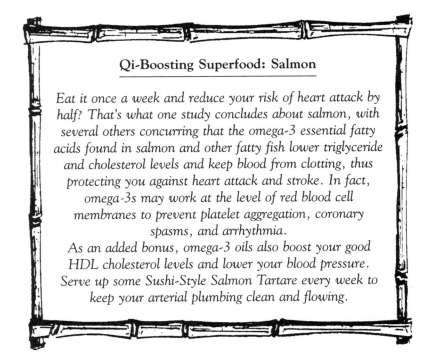

Qi-Boosting Superfood: Salmon

Eat it once a week and reduce your risk of heart attack by half? That's what one study concludes about salmon, with several others concurring that the omega-3 essential fatty acids found in salmon and other fatty fish lower triglyceride and cholesterol levels and keep blood from clotting, thus protecting you against heart attack and stroke. In fact, omega-3s may work at the level of red blood cell membranes to prevent platelet aggregation, coronary spasms, and arrhythmia.

As an added bonus, omega-3 oils also boost your good HDL cholesterol levels and lower your blood pressure. Serve up some Sushi-Style Salmon Tartare every week to keep your arterial plumbing clean and flowing.

Options and Opportunities

You can garnish the tartare with additional slices of pickled ginger and squiggles of wasabi (beware—it's hot!), or bring the seasonings to the table so everyone can combine to taste. This makes good finger food—simply pick up a nori square, roll it into a cylinder, and eat.

Complementary Elements

For a cool, make-ahead, high-flavor meal, serve the tartare as an appetizer and follow it with Rice Stick Noodle Salad.

The Feng Shui Plate

Compose a Five-Element plate and an interesting meal by placing the salmon in Fire's and Wood's guas at the top and left of the plate. In the center, make a mound of grated carrot salad dressed in rice vinegar and sugar. To the right, complement Metal with white sticky rice. And at the bottom, add a spoonful of salty black lumpfish roe.

Tempura du Jour

Yang

About 4–6 cups (1–1.5 l) total, your choice
  Zucchini, summer squash, Japanese eggplant, carrots, sweet potatoes, red potatoes, sliced thick
  Onions, sweet peppers, cut in chunks
  Green beans, scallions, cut into 2″ (5 cm) lengths
  Whole mushrooms, domestic or shiitake (remove tough stems)

About 1 pound (450 g) total, your choice
  Shelled raw shrimp, whole
  Calamari rings
  Raw chicken, beef, pork, firm fish fillets, cut into ½″ (1.25 cm) chunks

The Dipping Sauce
1½   cups (375 ml) water
1½   teaspoons instant dashi (Japanese soup stock)
¼   cup (60 ml) mirin (sweet Japanese cooking wine)
6   tablespoons soy sauce

6   cups (1.5 l) vegetable oil
  Flour (about 1½ cups, or 375 ml)
4–5   cups (1–1.2 l) panko (Japanese bread crumbs)

The Batter
2   eggs
½   cup (125 ml) water
1   teaspoon salt

1   lemon, cut in wedges

1. Prepare the vegetables, meat, and/or seafood of your choice as specified. Make sure all ingredients are dry.
2. Prepare the dipping sauce: Combine the water, instant dashi, mirin, and soy sauce in a saucepan and bring to a boil. Reduce the heat and keep warm over lowest heat.
3. Heat the oil in a wok, deep-fryer, or large, heavy pan to 340° to 360° F (170 to 182° C). Meanwhile, place some flour and some panko in 2 shallow, rimmed dishes for dredging and line a wire rack with paper towels for draining the tempura. Make the batter by lightly beating the eggs in a bowl, then beating in the water and salt.
4. To cook the tempura, work with one type of ingredient at a time. Dredge in flour and shake off the excess. Dip in batter and shake off the excess. Roll in panko and fry, turning once, until golden brown and tender, about 3 to 5 minutes (this will vary with the ingredient size and oil temperature). Remove with a slotted spoon and drain on the towel-lined rack. Skim stray pieces of batter from the oil as you go.
5. Serve the tempura with the dipping sauce in small individual bowls with lemon wedges alongside.

Serves 4.

The Essence of the Dish

Nothing heats you up like working fast over deep-frying food, so be sure you crave yang when you take on Tempura du Jour. Fried foods epitomize the richness and high temperature of yang energy, as you'll discover when you bite into that blistering nugget fresh from the pan without letting it cool for a moment first. You're playing with fire and boiling oil here, and that's the kind of game that brings out your assertion, quick response, and bravado. Try Tempura du Jour to prime yourself for multitasking and thinking on your feet.

Options and Opportunities

The dish is structured to be flexible, mixing and matching whatever ingredients you have on hand, what's fresh at the market, or the flavors you crave today. Tempura du Jour can be different every time you make it, exercising your creative muscle and providing constant challenge and stimulus to your yang force field. If you choose an all-vegetarian tempura (a great way to get meatless yang energy), double the quantity of vegetables. Use regular bread crumbs if you can't find panko.

Be sure to allow plenty of time for the oil to heat up. For efficient assembly-line production, dredge all of one type of ingredient in the flour. Dip one piece at a time in the batter and roll in the panko, leaving the pieces in the panko dish until all are coated. Working quickly, drop the pieces individually into the oil so that they don't stick together. Don't crowd the pan; if necessary, divide large batches in half. Transfer drained batches to a plate and keep warm in the oven at the lowest setting as you finish frying.

Complements
Beer is the classic drink to accompany tempura. After the heat of the deep-fryer, you'll probably be grateful for a simple dessert of fresh fruit, perhaps with a dollop of fat-free frozen yogurt. Or try Green Tea Tofu Flans, made in advance and chilled.

The Feng Shui Plate
Place the lemon wedge on the sour left side of Wood; place the dipping sauce at the bottom, in Water's dark and salty gua; and scatter the tempura over the rest of the plate.

THAI TACOS

Yang

2   tablespoons fresh lime juice
4   teaspoons fish sauce
1   teaspoon sugar
1   tablespoon peanut oil
1   pound (450 g) ground pork
1   tablespoon soy sauce
2   shallots, halved vertically and sliced lengthwise
1   scallion, sliced
1   fresh red chili pepper, halved, seeded, and sliced thin
1   tablespoon minced fresh ginger
1   tablespoon chopped fresh basil
¼   cup (60 ml) coarsely chopped roasted peanuts
1   small head butter lettuce, separated into leaves

1. Combine the lime juice, fish sauce, and sugar in a small bowl; stir to dissolve. Set aside.
2. Heat a wok or skillet over high heat and add the oil. When it's hot, add the ground pork, chopping and stirring to break it up, about 3 minutes. Add the soy sauce and stir-fry until the pork is just cooked, about 5 minutes more. Add the shallots, scallion, chili pepper, and ginger and continue to cook until fragrant and brown, about 3 minutes more.
3. Remove from the heat and stir in the lime juice mixture, basil, and peanuts.
4. At the table, spoon the pork into lettuce leaves, roll up, and eat.

   Serves 4 to 5 as a first course, or 2 to 3 as an entrée.

The Essence of the Dish

Spicy, sour, sweet, and salty, Thai Tacos present a good elemental mix as they please and

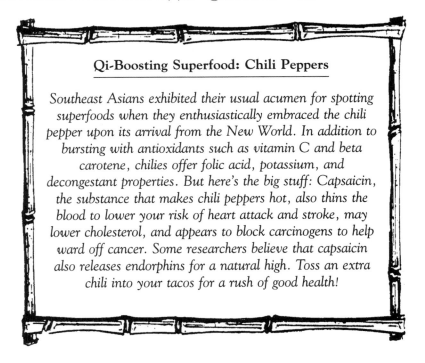

Qi-Boosting Superfood: Chili Peppers

Southeast Asians exhibited their usual acumen for spotting superfoods when they enthusiastically embraced the chili pepper upon its arrival from the New World. In addition to bursting with antioxidants such as vitamin C and beta carotene, chilies offer folic acid, potassium, and decongestant properties. But here's the big stuff: Capsaicin, the substance that makes chili peppers hot, also thins the blood to lower your risk of heart attack and stroke, may lower cholesterol, and appears to block carcinogens to help ward off cancer. Some researchers believe that capsaicin also releases endorphins for a natural high. Toss an extra chili into your tacos for a rush of good health!

tease your taste buds. The chili pepper's heat boosts Metal's influence, so expect a dose of righteousness—and the complementary Water energy in the pork gives you the clarity of mind to put your principles into perspective. The contrast between the warm, rich filling and the cool, tender lettuce wrapper reminds you of the importance of balance—and the messy juices prevent Metal and yang from making you too proud.

Options and Opportunities
Remember to have everything chopped before you start the stir-fry. If you don't eat pork, you can make the tacos with ground turkey instead.

Complements

When you're in a hurry, Thai Tacos make a quick, one-dish meal, a salad and entrée in one. For a more elaborate, hot-and-cold meal, serve the tacos as a first course with Five-Element Peanut Noodles. Try a tropical-fruit-style Chardonnay such as a Jekel Gravelstone alongside.

Desserts

Banana Coconut Cream Pudding

Yin

1   14-ounce (400 ml) can coconut milk
½   cup (125 ml) sugar
2   tablespoons (30 ml) cornstarch
    Pinch salt
4   egg yolks
½   teaspoon vanilla extract
1   banana, peeled and thinly sliced
½   cup (60 ml) orange juice

1. In a medium saucepan, bring the coconut milk to a boil, reduce the heat, and cook at a low boil for 3 minutes. Remove from the heat.
2. In a small mixing bowl, blend the sugar with the cornstarch and salt. Beat in the egg yolks. Whisk a little of the hot coconut milk into the egg mixture to temper, then add the mixture back into the saucepan. Cook over medium heat, whisking constantly, until the mixture is very thick and the whisk leaves a clear trail, 8 to 12 minutes. Remove from the heat and stir in the vanilla. Cool, cover, and chill.

3. Up to several hours before serving time, divide the custard among 4 dessert bowls. Dip the banana slices into the orange juice to prevent discoloration and arrange over the top of the puddings. Chill until you're ready to serve.

Serves 4.

The Essence of the Dish
This cool, silky pudding topped with soft bananas is pure comfort food, capable of whisking you back to the womb with one bite. With the sweet yellow banana a harbinger of Earth—honesty, faith, and wonder—this is a dessert to return you to a state of innocence.

Options and Opportunities
Be sure to use regular coconut milk, not cream of coconut. To prevent a skin from forming on the custard as it cools, place a piece of plastic wrap directly on the surface.

Complements
The pudding comes with a fairly high saturated-fat price tag, so your body will welcome it most after an unsaturated vegetarian meal such as Miso Soup, Rice Stick Noodle Salad, Soba Noodle Platter, Broccoli Bowties, Grilled Tofu Sandwich, Yin-Yang Salad, or a meatless Flexible Stir-Fry.

The Feng Shui Plate
Sweet, yellow, and filling the bowl from the center out, Banana Coconut Cream Pudding naturally nestles into the position of Earth.

BERRY BALSAMIC PARFAITS

Yin

½ cup (125 ml) balsamic vinegar
2 tablespoons sugar
1½ cups (375 ml) sliced strawberries
¾ cup (180 ml) blackberries
¾ cup (180 ml) blueberries

1. Combine the balsamic vinegar and sugar in a small saucepan, place over medium heat, and cook until reduced by 1/2 and syrupy, about 10 to 15 minutes. Cool.
2. Layer 1/2 the strawberries in the bottom of 4 glass dessert bowls or tall glasses. Top with a layer of all the blackberries, the remaining strawberries, and the blueberries. Drizzle the balsamic reduction over the top.
3. Cover the parfaits and chill until ready to serve.

Serves 4.

The Essence of the Dish

A textbook example of sweet-and-sour balance, Berry Balsamic Parfait is an elegant way to enjoy the best of summer's fruits. Vinegar is considered cooling and cleansing (and is recommended after childbirth), and this tart balsamic reduction teases out the sweetest nuance of the fruit's flavor for a Wood-and-Earth effect that detoxifies and nourishes, concentrates and relaxes your qi.

Your cells and digestive equipment will be happy, too. Superfruit strawberries are loaded with vitamin C (you get your daily value in about 3/4 cup, or 180 ml), along with potassium and the anticarcinogenic phytochemicals ellagic acid and flavonoids. And blackberries boast the highest fiber content of any berry.

Options and Opportunities

You can substitute raspberries for the blueberries or blackberries if either is unavailable or low in quality. Slice the strawberries lengthwise for an alluring heart shape.

Complements

This dessert complements any entrée, but would be particularly welcome as a balancing note after something rich or hot such as Fire-Roasted Filet Mignon or Drunken Firepot Shrimp.

BLACK BROWNIES

Yang

1   cup (250 ml) walnuts
6   ounces (170 g) unsweetened chocolate
½   cup unsalted butter (1 stick, or 125 ml), cut in pieces
2   cups (500 ml) sugar
1   tablespoon instant espresso or coffee
2   teaspoons black pepper
   Dash salt
3   eggs
1   teaspoon vanilla extract
1   cup (250 ml) flour

1. Preheat the oven to 350° F (177° C). Line a 13 × 9-inch (33 × 23 cm) baking pan with foil, add a little butter, and put this in the preheating oven for a minute or two to melt. Remove and rub the butter all over the foil with a paper towel. Set aside.
2. Toast the walnuts in the oven just until fragrant, 5 to 8 minutes. Chop coarsely.
3. Combine the chocolate and butter in a large microwaveable bowl and microwave on high for 2 minutes. Stir. If the chocolate is not yet melted, continue at 1-minute intervals, stirring in between. (Or melt the chocolate and butter together over simmering water in a double boiler.)
4. Stir the sugar, espresso powder, black pepper, and salt into the chocolate mixture. Stir in the eggs and vanilla. Add the flour and walnuts and stir just to combine.
5. Spread the batter in the prepared pan and bake until just set and a toothpick comes out with wet crumbs clinging to it, about 24 to 26 minutes. Cool completely, invert, peel off the foil, and cut into squares.

Makes 24 small or 12 large brownies.

The Essence of the Dish

Chocolate is sweet yang, and when it combines with bitter espresso and the punch of black pepper, it makes a dark brownie that will wake up your senses and cure the deepest of cravings. Rich and stimulating, chocolate is known to release endorphins in the body, like athletic activity—but without the sweat and strain.

With a four-element creative cycle—Fire from bitter chocolate and coffee, Earth energy in sweet sugar, Metal in the hot spice of the peppercorns, and Water from the brownies' black color—Black Brownies provide yang energy for any get-up-and-go venture.

Options and Opportunities

Lining the pan with foil enables you to remove the entire cake for easier cutting (this also spares the surface of your pan). The amount of black pepper called for here provides a subtle spice; you can adjust it up or down to your taste. If you prefer a thicker brownie, bake in a 9-inch (23 cm) square pan instead, allowing some extra baking time.

Complements

What doesn't go with chocolate? Try a perfectly balanced picnic with yin Rice Stick Noodle Salad and Black Brownies for dessert . . . or have a yang cookout with some Chili-Honey Barbecued Baby Back Ribs . . . or indulge your wildest yang fantasies with Fire-Roasted Filet Mignon With Wild Mushroom Sauce, saving a little red wine to sip with the brownies.

The Feng Shui Plate

Powerful, portable, and invested with many elemental forces, Black Brownies can be served however you like—in a napkin by the beach or on a beautiful glass dessert plate with a fork.

Fire and Ice Sundaes

Balanced

6 ounces (170 g) bittersweet chocolate, coarsely chopped
1 tablespoon unsalted butter
½ teaspoon instant espresso or coffee
¼ cup (60 ml) light corn syrup
¼ cup (60 ml) milk
1 quart (1 l) vanilla ice cream or frozen yogurt
¼ cup (60 ml) bourbon, warmed

1. Combine the chocolate and butter in a microwave- and heat-proof bowl and microwave on high for 1 minute. Stir. Continue at 30-second intervals until the chocolate is melted. Add the espresso or coffee, then gradually stir in the corn syrup, then the milk.
2. Serve the ice cream into bowls. At the table, ignite the bourbon and pour it into the sauce. When the flames die down, stir and spoon over the ice cream.

Serves 4, with leftover sauce.

The Essence of the Dish

Few dishes illustrate the concept of balance between opposites as graphically as Fire and Ice Sundaes. Ice cream and frozen yogurt are cold, sweet yin foods that relieve tension and anxiety by relaxing and expanding the stomach. Chocolate, coffee, and bourbon are all warming, bitter foods that stimulate the heart and liver, increasing energy and circulation. Hot and cold, black and white, stimulating and soothing, yang and yin—the marriage of burning chocolate to frozen vanilla is as exquisite as it is short lived. The melting ice cream in your bowl reminds you that perfect balance is always transitory, destined to give way to change and the start of a new cycle.

Options and Opportunities

You can substitute blended whiskey or Scotch for the bourbon. You can also vary the ice cream flavor, but at the expense of the purity of the chocolate-vanilla dichotomy. Be sure to serve the sundaes as fast as you can!

Complements

Fire and Ice Sundaes make a showstopping finish to any meal. Try them for all your special occasions.

The Feng Shui Plate

Clear glass bowls set off the yin-yang color scheme the best.

FIVE-SPICE ALMOND CAKE   Yang

4   ounces (120 g) blanched almonds (about 1 cup, or 250 ml)
3   tablespoons sugar
⅓   cup (80 ml) flour
½   teaspoon ground cinnamon
½   teaspoon ground ginger
½   teaspoon ground cloves
¼   teaspoon anise seeds, crushed
¼   teaspoon fennel seeds, crushed
3   eggs
⅔   cup (160 ml) sugar
2   teaspoons vanilla extract
½   teaspoon almond extract
⅛   teaspoon salt
½   cup (1 stick, or 125 ml) unsalted butter, softened

The Frosting

½   cup (1 stick, or 125 ml) unsalted butter, softened
½   cup (125 ml) sugar
½   teaspoon almond extract
½   cup (125 ml) warm milk

1. Preheat the oven to 350° F (177° C). Butter a 9-inch (23 cm) cake pan, line the bottom with wax paper, butter the paper, then coat with flour.
2. Grind the almonds and 3 tablespoons sugar in a food processor until well pulverized. Mix with the flour and spices and set aside.
3. Combine the eggs and 2/3 cup (160 ml) sugar in the top part of a double boiler, set over almost-simmering water, and beat at high speed with an electric mixer until the eggs

are foaming, thickened, and lightened in color, about 4 minutes. Remove from the heat, add the extracts and salt, and continue beating until the mixture is quite thick, smooth, and white, and forms a ribbon from the beaters, about 6 minutes more.

4. In a mixing bowl, beat 1 stick of the butter with a rubber spatula until fluffy. Using the spatula, fold in about 1/4 of the egg mixture, then 1/4 of the almond mixture. Repeat 3 times. Pour into the prepared pan and bake until golden brown, springy to the touch, and starting to pull away from the sides of the pan, 30 to 35 minutes.

5. Cool the cake in the pan on a rack for 15 minutes, then run a knife around the edge and invert onto the rack. Peel off the wax paper, reinvert onto another rack, and cool completely.

6. For the frosting, beat the butter and sugar together at high speed until light and fluffy. Beat in the almond extract. Very slowly beat in the warm milk.

7. Frost the top of the cooled cake, cover, and refrigerate overnight.

Serves 6 to 8.

The Essence of the Dish

This cake offers the heat and strength of yang in its buttery richness, warm spices, and the pure white of the almonds and frosting. Worried about the fat count? Well, don't eat it by the pound—but pleasure has been shown to keep people well, controlled indulgence tends to lead to better eating habits, and almonds are known to bring good fortune. The wise understand the power of a delicious dessert and exercise it with gleeful discretion.

Options and Opportunities

This is a classic Genoise cake, and its leavening comes from the structural changes enacted in eggs when beaten over heat. You'll need to exercise some patience with this step, but consider it entertainment: It's fascinating to watch the eggs metamorphose as air, heat, and agitation transform what is wet and dense into something dry and ascendant. Make sure your butter for the cake is very well softened or you'll run into mixing problems.

This cake is best the day after baking, when it has developed its full flavors. For a more festive look, decorate the top of the cake with toasted almonds and tidbits of candied ginger.

Complements
Want yang? The complex richness of this cake is a nice follow-up to something bright and brash such as Thai Tacos. Or perhaps you'd like an all-white, yin-yang luncheon of Crab and Cucumber Salad and cake.

The Feng Shui Plate
This becomes true good-luck cake when you activate the Metal in its white color and spicy ginger by serving it with the thick end of the wedge positioned to the right. Metal's forceful life energy reverses ill fortune and brings good luck to the entire household.

GREEN TEA TOFU FLANS

Yin

1½ cups (375 ml) plain soy beverage
1 bag green tea
7 ounces (260 g) regular tofu (½ block), patted dry
4 eggs
¾ cup (180 ml) sugar
1 teaspoon vanilla extract
Boiling water

1. Preheat the oven to 350° F (177° C).
2. In a small saucepan, heat the soy beverage over medium-high heat until it's scalding (just starting to bubble around the edges). Remove from the heat, add the tea bag, and steep for 6 minutes. Remove the tea bag and discard.
3. Place the tofu in a food processor and puree until smooth. Add the eggs and sugar and process. Add the infused soy milk and the vanilla and process until well combined.
4. Pour the custard into 6 (8-ounce, or 125 ml) custard cups. Place the cups in a baking pan and add 1 inch (2.5 cm) boiling water. Bake until just set, 50 minutes.
5. Cool the flans, chill, and invert onto serving plates.

Serves 6.

The Essence of the Dish

Take a chance on this unusual dessert, which is as delicious and healthful as you could wish. Dairy-free and low in fat, it's nonetheless smooth and creamy. Both tofu and green tea are superfoods linked with longevity. The sweet Earth simplicity of Green Tea Tofu Flan is a welcome antidote if you're congested—stressed or restless—and can prevent you from being selfish or stingy.

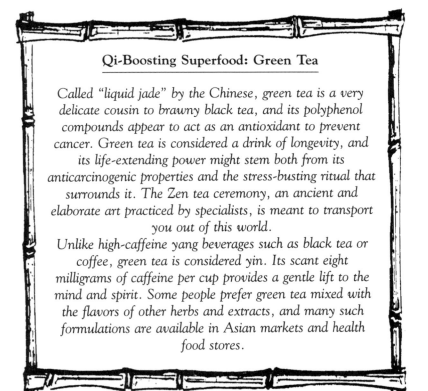

Qi-Boosting Superfood: Green Tea

Called "liquid jade" by the Chinese, green tea is a very delicate cousin to brawny black tea, and its polyphenol compounds appear to act as an antioxidant to prevent cancer. Green tea is considered a drink of longevity, and its life-extending power might stem both from its anticarcinogenic properties and the stress-busting ritual that surrounds it. The Zen tea ceremony, an ancient and elaborate art practiced by specialists, is meant to transport you out of this world.

Unlike high-caffeine yang beverages such as black tea or coffee, green tea is considered yin. Its scant eight milligrams of caffeine per cup provides a gentle lift to the mind and spirit. Some people prefer green tea mixed with the flavors of other herbs and extracts, and many such formulations are available in Asian markets and health food stores.

Yin-Yang Butterfly Dessert for Peak Sexuality

With a slight variation, this dessert becomes a recipe for love—a sexy finish to dinner that can enhance the biomechanics of the erotic equation. For the Yin-Yang Butterfly Dessert, omit the green tea from the flan and add 1 cup (250 ml) canned pumpkin (pureed with the tofu), increase the sugar to 1 cup (250 ml), and add 1 teaspoon ground cinnamon, 1/2 teaspoon ground ginger, and 1/4 teaspoon ground cloves along with the sugar. (You'll probably need an extra custard cup or two to accommodate the batter.) Serve the flan with a few squares of high-quality chocolate alongside.

Here are the sensual secrets of the Butterfly: For the woman, soy has been shown to increase lubrication where it counts. For the man, the aroma of baking pumpkin pie has been proven to enhance erections. For both partners, the Earth energy of pumpkin keeps you faithful, while chocolate's phenylethylamine compounds stimulate the nervous system, increase blood pressure and heart rate, and release endorphins—aphrodisiac processes that physically prepare you for the act of love. Chocolate is also yang to the flan's yin, providing the male-female balance essential to a successful liaison.

To preserve the pumpkin aroma, bake the flans on the same day as your dinner and keep the windows closed. Don't chill the flans; simply cool them and serve at room temperature.

Options and Opportunities

This recipe is lightly sweetened to let the delicate flavor of the tea shine through. If you have more of a sweet tooth, you might want to increase the sugar to 1 cup (250 ml).

Complements

The protein contributions of tofu and eggs makes this a particularly good finish to a vegetarian meal.

The Feng Shui Plate

Sweet and lightly golden, this embodiment of Earth should sit simply in the center of a small plate.

LIME PIE

Yin

      6 eggs
      ⅔ cup (160 ml) sugar
      ¾ cup (180 ml) fresh lime juice (about 6–7 limes)
      1 teaspoon minced lime zest
      4 tablespoons (½ stick) melted butter
      1 9″ (23 cm) graham cracker piecrust

1. Preheat the oven to 350° F (177° C). With an electric mixer, beat the eggs and sugar on high speed until light in color and slightly thickened. Reduce the speed to low and gradually blend in the lime juice and zest, then the melted butter.
2. Pour into the piecrust and bake for approximately 30 to 35 minutes, until the center is firm and the surface is dry to the touch.
3. Cool completely and chill until ready to serve.

      Serves 6 to 8.

The Essence of the Dish

Sour, green limes are the fruit of Wood, the element associated with family—and pie makes popular family fare. Wood further enhances the family dynamic by fostering loyalty and forgiveness, and by helping you face anger, an important process in any healthy group relationship.

Options and Opportunities

If you're using a piecrust in a thin aluminum pan, you can protect against spills by placing a baking sheet underneath before filling. If you have access to key limes from Florida, use them instead of regular limes for a classic Key Lime Pie.

Complements

The pure, intense tang of Lime Pie make it a good finish to any recipe in this book. Its bite offers a particularly nice contrast to entrées with a sweet edge, such as Mu Shu Chicken Wrap or Chili-Honey Barbecued Baby Back Ribs.

The Feng Shui Plate

Place each pie wedge in Wood's area on the left side of the plate, with the tip toward the center. You can garnish it with some strips of lime peel or fresh mint to reinforce the lime's green color, which is muted by the baking process. If you like, continue through the productive cycle with a few fresh raspberries or strawberries at the top of the plate to add a splash of Fire.

Recipes by Essential Nature— Yin, Yang, and Balanced

Yin

Asparagus, Spinach, and Shiitake Salad With Miso Dressing

Banana Coconut Cream Pudding

Berry Balsamic Parfaits

Chilled Tofu With Scallions and Sesame Oil

Crab and Cucumber Salad

Eggplant, Tomato, and Chevre Tart

Gingered Sweet Potato Soup

Grapefruit-Poached Sole With Watercress Sauce

Green Grape Gazpacho

Green Tea Tofu Flans

Lime Pie

Miso Eggplant

Miso Soup

Orange-Braised Tofu

Rice Stick Noodle Salad

Ruby Chicken Salad

Soba Noodle Platter

Soft Salad With Orange-Sage Vinaigrette

Stuffed Butternut Squash

Sushi-Style Salmon Tartare

Tamarind Cooler With Lime Cubes

Tomato Timbales With Avocado and Cream

Yang

Black Bean–Stuffed Chicken Breast
Black Brownies
Chicken and Daikon in Red Wine Sauce
Chili Oil
Chili-Honey Barbecued Baby Back Ribs
Drunken Firepot Shrimp
Fired-Roasted Filet Mignon With Wild
    Mushroom Sauce and Arugula Mashed
    Potatoes
Five-Spice Almond Cake
Fresh Ginger Tea
Lamb Satay With Peanut Sauce
Mending Moussaka
Pacific Martinis
Peppered Tuna With Wasabi Sauce
Quick Chickpea Curry
Sake-Glazed Black Cod With Ponzu Relish
Salt-Roasted Duckling With Beer-Braised
    Cabbage
Seared Salmon With Horseradish Butter
Sensuous Squab
Spicy Sesame Chicken
Tempura du Jour
Thai Tacos
White-Hot Cabbage Slaw

Balanced

Broccoli Bowties
Chicken Soup for a Cold
Chinese Chicken Salad
Coconut Shrimp Risotto
Crab With Ginger Beurre Brun
Fire and Ice Sundaes
Five-Element Peanut Noodles
Flexible Stir-Fry
Grilled Tofu Sandwich
Hot and Sour Mangoes
Lively Lentil Salad
Mu Shu Chicken Wrap
Oyster Egg Custard
Pineapple-Ham-Stuffed Yam
Pork and Shrimp Wontons With Cilantro
    Pesto
Sesame Pork Cellophane Noodles
Slimming Soup
Squid Ink Pasta With Calamari and
    Summer Vegetables
Warm Scallop Salad With Green Beans
    and Almonds
Yin-Yang Salad

Recommended Reading

Beinfield, Harriet. *Between Heaven and Earth: A Guide to Chinese Medicine*. New York: Ballantine Books, 1991.

Carper, Jean. *Food, Your Miracle Medicine: How Food Can Prevent and Cure Over 100 Symptoms and Problems*. New York: Harper Perennial Library, 1994.

Cost, Bruce. *Bruce Cost's Asian Ingredients: Buying and Cooking the Staple Foods of China, Japan, and Southeast Asia*. New York: William Morrow, 1988.

Duyff, Roberta Lawson. *The American Dietetic Association's Complete Food and Nutrition Guide*. Minnetonka, MN: Chronimed Publications, 1996.

English Chinese Dictionary of Medicine. San Francisco: China Books and Periodicals, 1979.

Le, Kim, Ph.D. *The Simple Path to Health: A Guide to Oriental Nutrition and Well-Being*. Portland, OR: Rudra Press, 1996.

Lip, Evelyn. *Feng Shui for the Home*. Torrance, CA: Heian International, 1995.

Needham, Joseph. *Science and Civilisation in China, Volume 3: Mathematics and the Sciences of the Heavens and the Earth*. Cambridge, England: Cambridge University Press, 1959.

Ritsema, Rudolf, and Stephen Karcher, translators. *I Ching, the Classic Chinese Oracle of Change: The First Complete Translation With Concordance*. Rockport, MA: Element, 1994.

Rossbach, Sarah. *Feng Shui: The Chinese Art of Placement*. New York: Arkana, 1983.

Tyler, Varro, Ph.D. *The Honest Herbal*. University, MS: Pharmaceutical Products Press, 1993.

Wilhelm, Richard, translator, and Cary F. Baynes, English translator. *The I Ching or Book of Changes*. Bollingen Series XIX. New York: Pantheon Books, 1950.

Williams, Tom, Ph.D. *The Complete Illustrated Guide to Chinese Medicine: A Comprehensive System for Health and Fitness*. Rockport, MA: Element, 1996.

Index